WOMANSWORD

WOMANSWORD

| What |
| Japanese |
| Words |
| Say |
| About |
| Women |

Kittredge Cherry

KODANSHA INTERNATIONAL
Tokyo • New York • London

For Audrey

Illustrations by Taro Higuchi.

Distributed in the United States by Kodansha America, Inc., 575 Lexington Avenue, New York, N.Y. 10022, and in the United Kingdom and continental Europe by Kodansha Europe Ltd., 95 Aldwych, London WC2B 4JF.

Published by Kodansha International Ltd., 17–14, Otowa 1-chome, Bunkyo-ku, Tokyo 112–8652, and Kodansha America, Inc.

First edition, 1987
First paperback edition, 1991
First trade paperback edition, 2002
LCC 86–40441
ISBN 4–7700–2888–1
02 03 04 05 06 07 08 09 10   10 9 8 7 6 5 4 3 2 1

www.thejapanpage.com

CONTENTS

2
Christmas Cake Sweepstakes:
GIRLHOOD TO WEDDING 37

3
Hey, Mrs. Interior:
MARRIED LIFE 55

4
Honor That Bag:
MOTHERHOOD   75

5
Office Flowers Bloom:
WORK OUTSIDE THE HOME   93

6
Pillow Talk:
SEXUALITY   107

7
Nice Middies Do:
AGING 125

Foreword

The woman/sword of Kittredge Cherry still cuts sharply in the Japan of the new millennium. While guided by a feminist perspective, her willingness to let go of preconception, combined with her keenly observant eye, leads her to shrewd insights into the ties between mother and son, the nonverbal communication of husband and wife, and much more.

Although the fundamentals of female identity, girlhood, marriage, motherhood, work, sexuality, and aging remain as Cherry described them, there has of course also been change as the country moved from the heady years of Japan as Number One in the eighties and early nineties to the bursting of the land speculation bubble and the so-called "lost decade" of economic stagnation, social disruption, and psychological uncertainty. In a more carefree Japan the emblematic bestsellers by women had been the stylish adaptation of traditional verse forms to the life and loves of an unmarried woman in *Salad Anniversary* by Machi Tawara, the amusing light essays of manga artist Momoko Sakura, and Banana Yoshimoto's *Kitchen* and other coming-of-age novels. Recently, by contrast, we have Mitsuyo Ohira's inspirational account (*Dakara, anata mo ikinuite* [You Too Can Live and Overcome]) of surviving school bullying (*ijime*), a suicide attempt, and life as a yakuza wife and then going on to become a lawyer, or the debut novel of Randy Taguchi (who emerged as an author via the Internet), titled *Konsento* (Electric Current), based on the life and death of her brother, who had been a *hikikomori*, or a young person psychologically unable to leave the house to go to school or work. Instead of novels like the 1987 *Norwegian Wood*, Haruki Murakami was at the close of the twentieth century doing a book of interviews with survivors of the poison gas attack on the Tokyo subway carried out by the Aum Shinrikyo cult.

Nowadays youth has become something of a fearful presence after several high-profile murders and other crimes by teenage boys—in one particularly horrific case, a fourteen-year-old boy killed an eleven-year-old acquaintance and placed his head in front of the school gate. There is also the unsettling new phenomenon of teen girls selling sex to middle-aged men in order to buy luxury goods, a practice euphemistically known as *enjo kosai* ("[financially] assisted dating"). Several new terms suggest that young people have become, if not necessarily frightening, at least harder for older generations to understand; these include *shinjinrui* ("new human species") and *oyayubizoku* ("thumb tribe," so named because of the speed with which they use their thumbs to type e-mails into their cell phones). Youth fashion also became more confrontational, as in multiple body piercings or the recent fads in which teenage girls adopted the looks known as *ganguro* ("black face," achieved by repeated visits to tanning salons and usually paired with hair dyed brown or blonde) and *yamamba* ("mountain witch," adding white lipstick and eyeshadow and frizzy bleached hair to the deep tan).

Japanese society also looks askance at young adults who are "parasite singles" or "freeters." The term parasite single (*parasaito shinguru*) was coined by a sociologist in 1995 to refer to young unmarried workers, then estimated at over half a million in number and seventy percent female, living at home with parents into their twenties and thirties and enjoying their wages as disposable income rather than marrying and buying consumer durables like refrigerators and, most importantly, having babies. The term freeter (*furitaa*) is a combination of the English word "free" with the last part of "arbeiter" (*arubaitaa*), from Arbeit, the German word for "work" that is used in Japan to refer to part-time or side jobs. Freeters are workers who do not settle into a regular job after graduation from high school or college but keep going from one temporary job to another. Widely regarded as slackers lacking a proper work ethic, freeters aged fifteen to thirty-four numbered 1.5 million in 1997 (out of sixty-five million employees overall).

However, blaming young people, especially women, for the continuing trends toward marrying later and having fewer or no children ignores the most common corporate response to economic contraction in Japan, which has been to protect older workers and to reduce labor costs by hiring only limited numbers of new graduates and providing generous early retirement packages. For the first time since the end of World War II incomes have stopped rising with each successive generation, and the gradual erosion of the paternalistic lifetime employment system is threatening the continued existence of the postwar family structure of single breadwinner and stay-at-home wife (*sengyo shufu*).

In addition, however, there are signs of a widening gap in the attitudes of young men and women. Many women do not want a marriage like the one their parents had, in which the father—devoted to his work—was an absentee husband and parent. On the other hand, despite calls a few years ago for fathers to take a more active role in parenting, many men are still resistant to change.

Equal opportunity employment laws have now opened the career path to women, making it an alternative to the established pattern in which a woman works as an OL ("office lady") at clerical duties, quits upon marriage or the birth of a child, and returns later to poorly paid part-time work after the children are older. The overall reduced hiring of new graduates under the prolonged economic slowdown, however, has resulted in limited entry of women to the corporate career track and increased exploitation of temporary workers, both male and female. Moreover, entering the career track at present means undertaking the same long hours and stress as men, in the country that gave us the word *karoshi*, death from overwork. If anything, the situation has worsened under threats of restructuring and redundancy, an increased workload after coworkers are let go and no replacements are hired, or transfer to another location. In fact depression and suicide have become significant problems among men in their fifties.

Under such conditions Japanese women, in effect, have to choose between having a career and having children, unless grandparents are available for childcare. Government white papers regularly mention the need for more day-care facilities, after-school programs for school-age children, and flexible working hours for both mothers and fathers, but little seems to have changed in practice yet. This may be due in part to the economic situation, but it is also undoubtedly the result of deeply held ideas that men should place duty (to the state in the prewar period and to the company in modern times) before private concerns and that for women there is no higher calling than to be a stay-at-home mom.

I will never forget a wedding reception I attended several years ago at which the groom, an employee at a large bank, was praised by coworkers for putting in long hours with them on a special project without ever even hinting that he'd like some time off to spend with his mother, who happened to be dying. Young mothers also sometimes snap (*kireru*) under the pressure of raising perfect children without the traditional support network of an extended family or any help from their husband, who often leaves the house at eight a.m. or earlier and doesn't return until around midnight.

Child abuse—or public recognition of it—has been on the rise. In a famous incident in 1999, a thirty-five-year-old housewife strangled a two-year-old girl whose brother attended the same Tokyo nursery school as her own child. At first the crime was regarded as a case of *ojuken satsujin* (entrance exam murder), because the victim had gained admittance to an elite kindergarten—the ticket to a prestigious elementary school, junior high school, high school, and college—while her own daughter had not. It emerged later, however, that stress in interpersonal relations was a primary factor. A nurse for ten years in Shizuoka before marrying and moving to Tokyo, the murderer had become friends with a neighborhood woman who had a son and daughter of the same ages as her own children. When that mother formed other friendships and seemed to slight her and her children, the woman decided to punish her by killing her child.

The social pressure on young mothers and the unhealthy concentration of energy on childraising can be seen in the ritualized phenomenon of the "park debut" (*koen debyuu*), in which young mothers and their children make their first, anxiety-filled visit to their local neighborhood park and endeavor to break into the hierarchical, closed society of the mother-and-children regulars who gather there. Park society can be notoriously cold to newcomers, leaving unfortunate parent-child teams isolated or forced to try their luck elsewhere. Some department stores have even sold special mom-and-child park debut outfits.

The difficulty of changing the system can be seen in recent attempts to introduce *yutori aru kyoiku* (education with latitude) to the Japanese school system. Well-meaning efforts to reduce rote memorization and foster creativity by streamlining the curriculum and reducing class hours (eliminating Saturday classes) have met with strong resistance from parents and local governments, who worry about lowered academic standards and about the children falling behind or having more time to get into trouble. Increased uncertainty about the future and the crumbling of social institutions seem to lead not to change but to a desperate clinging to older patterns and beliefs—and to cynicism, rebelliousness, and apathy among the young.

The falling birthrate is a contributing factor in the greying of Japanese society; in April 2002 the rate stood at 1.35 births per woman, well below the replacement level of 2.1 necessary to keep the numbers from declining. It is expected that in fifty years people aged sixty-five and over will constitute thirty-six percent of the population and that the population will start to shrink from 2004 or 2005. A book entitled *Rojinryoku* (Old Age Power) was a bestseller and a pair of hundred-year-old twin sisters, Kin-san and Gin-san, became media celebrities. Judging from the Kin-san/Gin-san phenomenon, it seems that even in old age Japanese society favors females being cute and cuddly (*kawaii*)! Indeed a few years ago a manga artist coined the term *obatarian* (a combination of *obasan* [auntie] and the movie *Batarian*, which is the Japanese title of the American horror film *Return of the Living Dead*). It refers to pushy middle-aged women who steamroller their way to the front of a line or bore steadily through a crowded train car in search of a seat. Somehow there doesn't seem to be a corresponding negative term to refer to the oblivious older men who sprawl out over more than their share of a train seat and share their disgusting personal hygiene habits (spitting, pulling out nose hairs, sneezing loudly without covering their mouth, etc.) with everyone around them.

Other developments since Cherry wrote include:

- Debate continues on the question of allowing married couples to have separate surnames (*fufu bessei*); in 1996 it was decided that a couple could use either the wife's or the husband's name, but that both still had to use the same name.
- In 1999 Viagra was approved in just six months, although the birth control pill had at that time been mired in testing and debate for twelve years. In fact outcry among women over Viagra's super-quick introduction to Japan seems to have finally been the catalyst for approval of the Pill.

- The birth of a daughter to the crown prince after eight years of marriage revived interest in the idea of making female heirs eligible for succession to the throne. In a startling departure from tradition, the oldest female member of Japan's royal family wrote an article in a popular monthly women's magazine expressing her support for the idea. Princess Kikuko, the ninety-year-old widow of the late Emperor Hirohito's younger brother, Prince Takamatsu, wrote in *Fujin Koron* (Women's Views) that there were precedents in Japan's history for the idea of a female monarch, and that nations such as Britain have thrived under the rule of a queen.
- Sexual harassment (known as *sekuhara*) was the subject of joking remarks for some time but after various court judgments in favor of victims it is now taken more seriously.
- Some train companies have established cars reserved for women (*josei sen'yo sharyo*) at certain times of day as a countermeasure against sexual molesters (*chikan*) but the primary tactic is still the Confucian use of moral exhortation, as in recent posters calling on everyone to "*Sutoppu za meiwaku!*" (Stop the public nuisance) or to say "*Chikan ni NO!*" (NO to *chikan*).
- Protests such as those Cherry mentions over the term "*joryu bungaku*" (ladies'/women's literature) led last year to the Joryu Bungaku Prize being renamed the Fujin Koron Bungei Prize; it will no longer be awarded only to woman novelists but to authors, male or female, of works related to women.
- The dearth of Japanese women willing to marry young Japanese farmers and live in rural areas has been overcome by bringing in foreign brides, mainly from other Asian countries.
- Gender preference for children in nonrural areas has shifted in recent years from boys to girls, who are regarded as easier to raise and more likely to look after elderly parents. In 1997 only twenty-five percent of respondents to one government survey wanted a boy.
- Young women continue to be perceived as *shokuba no hana* ("office flowers"), as seen in a recent photo-essay in a leading magazine that marveled at the presence of thirty-nine women employees in the main Tokyo subway system—of nearly 9,700 workers—declaring them a fresh breeze (*sawayaka na kaze*) for rush-hour commuters. On the other hand, women newscasters, whose role in the past was mainly decorative, have come to have a role more

equal to their male counterparts.

- Single mothers increased 20.9 percent in the period from 1993 to 1998, to 954,000 households; approximately eighty percent became single mothers as a result of divorce, but the number of unwed mothers has also been increasing. Single-father households numbered 163,400 and had roughly double the yearly income of single-mother families.

- The larger number of women working full-time has resulted in more married women spending several years in what is known as *tanshin funin*: accepting a company-ordered transfer to another part of the country and moving there alone for the duration of the appointment, leaving family behind to continue their work or schooling. The number of women in this situation rose to 900 in 1998 (as compared with 314,000 men).

Finally, in her preface Cherry writes about how she came to appreciate more fully the inner strength of Japanese women, so different from their image of subservience in the West. I too have been struck by their pragmatic strength and resilience. I don't know if it comes from a residue of Japanese matriarchy, as Cherry speculates, but I do know that Japanese women will very likely need all the strength they can find in what promises to be a trying period of transition in the years ahead.

Considering the social conservatism of a Japanese culture that discourages the formation of a public social welfare safety net and any significant immigration into Japan, it looks as if it might be Japanese women who will be called upon to simultaneously care for the elderly, help make up for any shortage of workers, and raise children. If Japanese men were the unsung heroes of the early postwar years, reconstructing Japan from the rubble of World War II, then Japanese women will be the quiet samurai of the new millennium, battling to construct new gender roles and family patterns to fit the new economic and demographic reality. Let us hope that, unlike the corporate samurai who often lost all identity except as company men, they will be able to hang on to that core identity so interestingly explored by Cherry and to skillfully balance their many challenging social and personal roles.

Janet Ashby
Tokyo, April 2002

Preface
to the Original Edition

Like many Japanese terms explained in *Womansword*, the title of this book has a double meaning. It can be pronounced "woman's word" to mean a woman's way of looking at words. Words are often used with the same nuances by and about both genders, but *Womansword* focuses on those that are not. This type of analysis can cut incisively to the heart of cultural assumptions, hence the alternate pronunciation, "woman sword." Its application to Japanese language is particularly appropriate, since women there have been parrying and slashing with actual swords since the seventeenth century. The daughters of samurai warriors were expected to master the use of a halberd called a *naginata* by age eighteen, both for exercise and so they could defend their home and their honor, fighting to the death if necessary. Today *naginata* swordplay continues to be the only martial art in Japan where women predominate. All of this I wanted to convey in the title, but no existing English word would do it. As I worked on the book, struggling to make one language explain another, I came to feel I deserved to create a word of my own.

My efforts to make sense of the contrast between Japanese and English words began shortly after I stepped off the plane at Narita Airport in 1982, a young American woman eager to conquer the Japanese language and Japanese sexism, not necessarily in that order. I remember finding a word in my bilingual dictionary that I thought would be a good way to introduce myself: "a spirited woman." But when I tried out *otoko masari* on a friend, she was horrified. "Nobody wants to be *that!*" she exclaimed. Such words provided a jumping-off point for discussions that soared far beyond so-called women's issues to how females and males relate to each other, and on to how Japanese culture works.

Our conversations often led Japanese of both genders to praise the strength of their nation's women. At first I was puzzled because this assertion flagrantly defies the evidence provided by some standard measures of women's status: wages, opportunities, access to birth control and child care. On all these counts, Japanese women rank low. They also tend to look weak in public: nodding agreement and bowing deeply, plying men with tea and service, demurely hiding their giggles behind their hands. Gradually I came to see that their strength is something internal, far removed from overt display. When women encouraged men to bask in public glory, it reminded me of the way they would indulge a child who craved a sweet-bean treat. In direct confrontation, the women may yield like blades of grass— and spring back just as quickly. One of them compared this flexibility to the Vietcong guerillas, who could not be eradicated by the greater might of the U.S. military.

Psychologically, Japanese women depend largely on each other. In their sex-segregated society, they could be criticized for living in a female ghetto, and yet they have what some American feminists are trying to build, a "women's culture" with its own customs, values, and even language.

Searching for the source of their strength, I was struck by something that the Japanese women themselves take for granted: the residue of the Japanese matriarchy. In ancient times, a matrilineal family pattern gave women greater political and religious power, which may have spilled over into other spheres as well. Historians still debate how a complex set of forces got the patriarchal revolution rolling: the gradual evolution of agriculture and the acceptance of Confucian and Buddhist views on women's inferiority. They estimate that the tide began to turn in favor of patriarchy during the Taika Reform in the second half of the seventh century, when Japan institutionalized many concepts that had been filtering over from China for several centuries. However, men never isolated Japanese women to the extent of Hindu purdah, nor crippled them with anything like Chinese foot binding, nor murdered them on the mass scale of the medieval European witch burnings. This may help explain why matriarchal influence can still be glimpsed in Japan. The sun goddess continues to be revered by Shinto followers. One custom enables a family to adopt a son-in-law who assumes his wife's surname and enters her family just as a bride would normally do. Another encourages a pregnant woman to leave her husband and stay with her mother while giving birth.

With language as my vehicle, I gradually came closer to understanding Japanese women. My best teachers have been the very words and the women who use them, splendidly ordinary and much like myself. In August 1983, I began writing monthly about these instructive words for a Tokyo-based feminist journal. While maintaining that column, I launched a similar one in a general-interest magazine about Japan in 1985. Even Japanese women said my approach awoke them to the gender-based assumptions built into their language. Their enthusiasm propelled me beyond my main reservation: shouldn't Japanese women, like all people, be speaking for themselves? What I can contribute is the vision of a woman who was raised in one society and lived in another, a bi-cultural perspective that people of both sides encouraged me to share.

From the wealth of colorfully telling expressions in Japanese, I chose those most closely related to women and most commonly used. My main criterion in deciding which words to include was their significance as I perceived it. Each and every word presented in these pages struck me as saying something about Japanese womanhood, and therefore about their society as a whole. Most of the terms I chose are used to describe girls, women, and their lives. However, to allow females to speak for themselves, I include a few words developed and used mostly by women to talk about their relationships with men, such as "giant garbage" (sodai gomi), slang for a retired husband.

These words are almost all readily recognized by Japanese women today, though some sound old-fashioned. The exceptions are a few ancient terms and some contemporary slang limited to certain segments of the population. Of course, each person's vocabulary is as unique as a fingerprint, so these definitions do not provide a perfect match for how any single individual uses the words. Unfamiliar words were included only if they seemed irresistibly revealing about women in Japan.

Some subjects, such as prostitution, generate more than their fair share of vivid expressions. I purposely weeded out redundant terms in order to present the broad vista of women's experience. This book does not attempt to be an exhaustive list of every Japanese word related to the female gender, but a savory stew with a bit of everything tossed in, seasoned by my own idiosyncrasies.

At the same time, explanations of Japanese grammar are beyond the scope of this book. I have done my best to make English glosses correspond to the part of speech in Japanese by providing a verb for a verb, a noun for a noun. But the difference in the languages makes precise translation impossible. The English equivalents at the top of each entry are often just that: approximations with a spicy flavor as opposed to precise renderings of terms that may be untranslatable puns or idioms. A full explanation of the wordplay, nuance, and background information is given in each essay, usually peppered by alternative expressions and salted with my own observations. It is especially important to be aware that Japanese lacks the distinction between singular and plural. I have taken the liberty of interchanging singular and plural glosses for a harmonious blend in English. Another potentially confusing feature of Japanese is pronunciation. Some consonants are voiced in compound words; for example, Japanese say *sato-gaeri* when they combine *sato* (hometown) and *kaeri* (return). Many Japanese ideograms, known as characters, have multiple pronunciations, divided generally into Chinese (*on*) readings and Japanese (*kun*) readings. I give the one appropriate for the usage described, and if a character is introduced with no particular context, I give a *kun* reading unless that would change the meaning.

If not otherwise indicated, statistics cited come from the Japanese government. An exchange rate of 150 yen per dollar is used to convert currency.

My collection of words seemed to cleave naturally into seven chapters according to subject matter. Within the chapters, each essay generally contains a variety of words, phrases, and proverbs clustered around a single theme, such as beauty or pregnancy. The book is designed so the reader can use it as a dictionary, with each essay containing enough background information to stand alone. Or an entire chapter can be read at one sitting to learn about a whole facet of women's lives.

Since my goal is to present the women-related aspects of Japanese language and culture to readers of English, I resisted the temptation to draw extensive comparisons with English expressions. This does not mean I overlook the bias in my own native tongue, only that I assume readers have the ability to recognize it for themselves, especially if they've been sensitized by contact with the Japanese language.

Everybody I ever talked to during my stay in Japan, whether female or not, Japanese or not, contributed to the understanding which led to this book, as did everyone who discussed Japan with me after my return to America. Some people deserve special mention in addition to my heartfelt gratitude for their help. Audrey E. Lockwood was a continual inspiration, even before she seized the opportunity to publish these vignettes in the monthly magazine she edited, *Feminist Forum*. The editors of *PHP Intersect* further encouraged me by publishing these items as "Telling Terms" starting in 1985. My ideas fused into an organized reality because my editors, Pamela Pasti and Michiko Hiraoka, dared to give me their confidence and their vision. Catherine Broderick and Gerry Harcourt urged me onward as they kept introducing me to more words and more Japanese women. Donald Philippi assisted me with historical words, especially the passage I quote from his translation of the *Kojiki*. Further information and insights came from Regina Garrick and her Ph.D. dissertation ("Juvenile Delinquency Among Japanese Girls," University of Tokyo, 1984). I am also grateful for the support of the International Women's Year Action Group and the International Feminists of Japan, as well as to my professors at International Christian University and Kobe College. Most of all, I want to thank the Japanese women who generously opened their hearts and shared their words: Misako Hamada, Ziggie Yoko Kato, Mayo Issobe, Michiko Ito, Kazuko Katsuta, Norimi Kawamoto, Eiko Kawatani, Teruko Kobayashi, Mariko Mitsui, Reiko Nakamura, Ikuyo Ohno, Keiko Shiraishi, Yoshiko Wada, and Mieko Watanabe. Last but not least is Kazue Suzuki, whose steadfast friendship and indomitable spirit became my guiding light in Japan.

JAPANESE HISTORICAL PERIODS	
Nara	646 — 794
Heian	794 — 1185
Kamakura	1185 — 1333
Nanbokucho	1333 — 1392
Muromachi	1392 — 1568
Momoyama	1568 — 1603
Edo	1603 — 1868
Meiji	1868 — 1912
Taisho	1912 — 1926
Showa	1926 — 1989
Heisei	1989 —

1

In the Beginning, Woman Was the Sun
FEMALE IDENTITY

Amaterasu Omikami Great Heaven-Shining Mother 天照大御神

On the first day of the new year, some Japanese awake early to watch the sun peep over the horizon, reminding them of their own origins. The sun goddess, the Great Heaven-Shining Mother (*Amaterasu Omikami*), is the foremother of all the Japanese people and the supreme deity in Shinto mythology. Shinto is one of the few religions in the world to perceive the sun as female. According to the myth first recorded about thirteen hundred years ago, Amaterasu gave her grandson the mirror, sword, and cashew-shaped jewels still venerated as the "Three Sacred Treasures," then sent him down to populate the "Land of Plentiful Reed-covered Plains and Fresh Rice Ears," starting with Japan. The present emperor traces his pedigree directly back to the sun goddess, boasting the world's longest unbroken succession.

Amaterasu and her sacred mirror are enshrined at the most holy Shinto shrine, the Grand Shrine of Ise. The shrine is so ancient that its origin is clouded in scholarly debate; its own brochures claim it was founded there in 4 B.C. by the princess Yamato-hime-no-Mikoto. Unlike most shrines, it is built in the oldest Japanese architectural style and presided over by a high priestess. This position, traditionally held by an imperial princess, was abolished in 1868 and revived in 1946. Although their highest deity is female, all but a few Shinto priests are men. They are assisted by many female attendants called *miko*.

While Shinto ignites unpleasant memories of militarism in some Japanese, her majesty the sun has long provided inspiration for Japanese women, including poet Hiratsuka Raicho. She founded a feminist literary circle called the Bluestocking (*Seito*) Society, a forerunner of contemporary feminist activism. To inaugurate the first issue of the group's journal *Bluestocking* in 1911, she harkened back to the myths starring Amaterasu. Raicho's poem, probably Japan's most famous feminist declaration, opens with the words "In the beginning, woman was the sun. An authentic person."

anegohada   Big-Sister Types   姉 御 肌

Big-sisterhood is powerful in Japan. Women usually are not viewed as both strong and good; they are one or the other unless they fall into a special category such as "big-sister skin" (*anegohada*). In this case, skin means nature or type. *Ane* is elder sister, and the *go* in between adds a layer of either respect or affection. A strong, honest, and capable woman of any age may be admired by men as well as women in Japan as an *anegohada*. The big-sister type leads and looks after her underlings on the job, at school, or anywhere else in a style Westerners might term "paternalistic." She will be kind to those younger or weaker than herself. She chooses protégés, not necessarily female, and may help them out and encourage them. To Japanese, this is big-sister behavior.

A sisterly benefactor can also be called "parent-role skin" (*oya-bunhada*), a word usually applied to men. Gangster societies, which nurse similarly powerful bonds between older ring leaders and younger henchmen, provide another context for the terms *anegohada* and *oyabunhada*. To gangsters, a big sister can be either the leader's wife or a female with the same leadership instinct displayed by *anegohada* in other walks of life.

At work or at home, older sisters are authority figures in Japan, where age always confers privilege and responsibility. The Japanese language doesn't even have a word that means just "sister" without specifying whether she is an older sister (*ane*) or a younger sister (*imoto*). The closest it comes is the plural *shimai* (sisters), a compound of the two characters. *Shimai* is also used for sister cities, allied companies, and the like. In the family, siblings address their older sisters politely as *oneesan*, while big sisters talk down to their younger siblings by using their given names. The words for older brother, younger brother, and brothers (*kyodai*) work the same way, except *kyodai* is also used generically to refer to both female and male siblings.

Anne no hi   Anne's Day   アンネの日

Once she recovered from the shock, Anne Frank would probably get a good laugh out of the way her name has been immortalized in Japan. "Today is Anne's Day (*Anne no hi*)," one woman might whisper to another. Her message is far removed from World War II and the Nazi regime that forced the Jewish teenager and her family into hiding. The diary Anne kept moved millions to ponder the insanity of war. It also gave Japan a now old-fashioned term for menstruation. Although few people say *Anne no hi* anymore, older women still recognize it and remember it when they speak, not of war and death, but of the flowing potential for life.

Anne broached this topic tenderly once: "Each time I have a period—and that has been only three times—I have the feeling that in spite of all the pain, the unpleasantness and nastiness, I have a sweet secret and that is why, although it is nothing but a nuisance to me in a way, I always long for the time that I shall feel that secret within me again."

The connection is so obscure that it would never have occurred to the average Japanese if it weren't for a certain sanitary napkin and tampon manufacturer that chose to call itself Anne Co., Ltd. This firm introduced the first paper sanitary products proportioned for Japanese women in 1961, using "Anne's Day" as an advertising theme. Japanese women were already familiar with such feminine protection, because these products were first imported to Japan shortly after Kimberly-Clark Corporation introduced its Kotex brand to America in 1921. In his memoirs, the Anne PR chief who helped christen the products notes the aim was to clean up the reputation of menstruation and related items: "The image we presented had to be beautiful, pure, not of suffering but of delight, not gloomy but bright."

With their uplifting ad campaign, the men of Anne may have been raising menstruation back to the lofty status it enjoyed long ago. Some scholars surmise that in ancient times Japanese women were considered unapproachable during menstruation because it was seen as a sign of being sacred to the gods. This belief may have been behind one of the world's first recorded poems about menstruation, which appears in Japan's oldest book, the *Kojiki*, completed in 712. A warrior has just returned from heroic exploits, ready to wed his beloved princess, when he spots menstrual blood on her clothes. Perhaps because it means she is too holy to touch, he laments, "Although I desire to sleep with you, on the hem of the cloak you are wearing the moon has risen" (*tsuki tachinikeri*). This ancient euphemism is also used by the princess, who quickly shifts the blame to the man for being away so long: "It is no wonder that while waiting in vain for you, on the cloak I am wearing the moon should rise."

In later centuries, there is no question that menstruation came to be viewed as pollution. Menstruation is said to be *kegarawashii*, or filthy, disgusting, obscene. The receptacles for sanitary napkins in public rest rooms sometimes are still labeled with this potently filthy character, in this case in a compound word pronounced either *obutsu* or *yogoremono*. The traditional exception to this dismal attitude was a girl's first menstrual period, a rite of passage celebrated with merrymaking methods that varied from one region to another. For example, in one corner of Shizuoka Prefecture, neighbors presented a bag of rice and said, "A new flower has bloomed, congratulations!" Word of the momentous event spread quickly through the neighborhood when the woman-child made her first trip to the hut where women were isolated during that time of the month.

First-period festivities are disappearing, while euphemisms continue to thrive. Women disguise menstruation linguistically with polite circumlocutions such as the old-fashioned "monthly obstacle" (*tsuki no sawari*), which can also denote a cloud over the moon. The most common euphemisms are the medical term *seiri* (physiology), the English borrowing *mensu*, *gekkei* (period), and just plain *are* (that). An outmoded but colorful slang term is "rising sun" (*hi no maru*), a pun on the Japanese "rising sun" flag: a red circle on a field of white. It took a satirical wit to link menstruation with the patriotic symbol; prior to World War II, nationalism was almost synonymous with state Shinto, a religion that included the concept of menstruation as contamination.

bijin Beauties   美人

Beauty is female. "I met a beauty today" generally means the speaker encountered a beautiful woman. Likewise, the Japanese talk about meeting a *bijin*, literally "beauty-person" but actually used exclusively for beauties of the female persuasion. In contrast, gender is usually specified in the various words for male beauties, such as "beauty-man" (*binan*).

The term can be affixed to almost any job title to forge compounds denoting such Japanese phenomena as the "beauty-announcer" (*bijin anaunsaa*) delivering the TV news, the "beauty-hostess" (*bijin hosutesu*) serving drinks in hostess clubs, and even the "beauty-editor" (*bijin henshusha*) working on books like this one. In the old days, about a thousand years ago, a *bijin* had a special job reserved just for her. Early written records indicate that villagers used to do their saké-making through a primitive fermentation process that began with chewing rice and spitting the wad into a large wooden tub. The purity of the saké was ensured by allowing the rice to be chewed only by *bijin*—in this case meaning young virgins. The resulting wine was appropriately called *bijinshu*, or "beauty saké."

Nowadays good looks are still an important job qualification for females. The expression "graceful figure" (*yoshi tanrei*) keeps popping up in help-wanted ads for women. This blend of style and beauty is a stated requirement for such positions as tour guide, showroom product demonstrator, and receptionist, and an unwritten rule for many other jobs open to women. The characters themselves conceivably could apply to an attractive male figure, but common usage denies this interpretation. Employers value men more for their inner qualities, and seldom advertise for fine male physiques. Likewise, the words for good-looking guys cannot be made into compounds with their job titles.

They may find employment with relative ease, but beautiful women are considered more likely than their plain sisters to suffer misfortunes and even untimely death. As a common proverb puts it, "Beauties are short-lived" (*Bijin hakumei*). The adage also hints at the impermanence of youthful prettiness and the fact that Japanese tend to perceive transience itself as beautiful. The national passion for cherry blossoms is partly based on the fact that they fade so quickly.

Standards of beauty are fleeting, too, as can be seen by glancing back through a few centuries of Japanese art, especially the genre of ukiyo-e known as "beauty pictures" (*bijinga*). One era's beauty is another's beast. Black teeth, once an essential part of personal grooming for women, provoke disgust today. Fashion shifts back and forth from round, plump-cheeked faces to the longish ovals hailed as "melon-seed faces" (*urizane-gao*). In the Edo period, men wrote of their desire for a young woman with a small mouth, eyebrows like a crescent moon rising in the mist over a distant mountain, hair like the wing of a wet crow, and a "Mount Fuji forehead" (*Fuji-bitai*). This old-fashioned phrase was suggested by the pointed shape of the hairline that English speakers call a widow's peak.

Traditionally, a Japanese woman's appeal was said to reside in an anatomical part that most other nations ignore: the nape (*unaji*) of the neck. More than breasts, buttocks, or legs, the nape exuded sensuality. The reason behind the beguilingly elusive aesthetic was simple. The rest of her physique was cloaked by kimono. Even her nape was often hidden beneath her ebony mane, so when a woman put up her hair, it caused the same delicious pitter-pat that Westerners may feel when they spot a woman in a low-cut dress. Nape appreciation is on the decline, but it was still strong enough in the mid-1980s for a popular women's magazine to run a feature on *unaji bijin* with shots of stars flaunting their napes.

Japanese claim the nape's allure is far more subtle than the Western breast fixation, perhaps closer to the magnetism of an exquisite smile. Breasts, colloquially called *oppai* or *chichi*, never used to be sexual targets in Japan, where mothers breast-fed babies in public until about thirty years ago. Provincial women stripped to the waist when they worked, until defeat in World War II brought gawking U.S. soldiers to the country. Laws allowing breasts to be shown on television with impunity are a remnant of past attitudes, but the titillating nature of many such broadcasts is a sign that the Western fetish seems to have taken hold. Despite the new trends, many Japanese men confide in secrecy that big breasts are overwhelming—even scary.

Rice-cake skin (*mochi hada*) is another attribute admired by the Japanese, who are well acquainted with just how soft, smooth, white, and utterly delightful a pounded-rice cake can be. The key here is whiteness, for a popular Japanese proverb decrees, "White hides seven defects" (*Iro no shiroi wa shichi nan kakusu*), meaning a pale complexion compensates for a large mouth or a flat nose or a myriad of other imperfections.

Japanese women began using a face and body powder called "the honorable white" (*oshiroi*) along with other cosmetics more than a thousand years ago in an effort to personify this ideal. The earliest type of powder, made of rice flour and soil, was supplanted by lead-based powder imported from China in the seventh century. Its poisonous nature was recognized in the 1870s, and a lead-free version was developed, only to be replaced by Western-style make-up foundation. Men also painted their faces to enhance their attractiveness in the Heian period. Gradually make-up application became a feminine pursuit, although in the mid-1980s, Japan's leading cosmetics firms began offering lines of make-up foundation, lipsticks, and eyebrow pencils for men, along with classes on how to use them.

What the white couldn't cover up, proper deportment could, according to a nineteenth-century Japanese bestseller on how to be a beauty. Its recommendations include this advice for women who wanted their eyes to look narrower: Focus on a spot two yards from your feet when standing, half as far when seated. Today some women take more drastic action—cosmetic surgery—to match the current ideal. The three most common of such operations undergone by Japanese women are what is called "Westernization" of the upper eyelid, building up a flat nose, and improving the chinline.

busu Uglies   ブ ス

The Japanese subtitle says "*Busu!*" when actor Dustin Hoffman fights with his girlfriend in *Tootsie* and utters the ultimate English obscenity, "Fuck you!" These nasty words are parallel only in certain situations, because *busu* means a woman with a hideous face. It is one of the worst Japanese insults that can be hurled at a female, though it can also be a tease, possibly even for a boyfriend or a pet. The ugly woman called *busu* in Japan would probably be dismissed as a "dog" by English speakers.

People are often likened to animals in English, but Japanese seldom make such comparisons. One of the few is a milder and slightly old-fashioned jibe for a plain-looking female: literally "fawning turtle" (*okame*). Still, Japanese usually do not connect it with the tortoise of the animal kingdom. *Okame* is a name for the female half of the ubiquitous pair of traditional Kyogen comedy masks found in most Japanese tourist shops. Her goofy countenance with its vast expanse between eyes and eyebrows is unforgettable, and Japanese have adopted her name as a taunt. Some Japanese historians theorize that when the first *Okame* masks were fashioned long ago, her plump, turtlelike face was considered ideal. A contemporary Kyogen actor once summed up her vapidly giddy expression as what every Japanese guy hopes his bride will look like on his wedding night.

Rooted in a long agricultural tradition, Japanese culture draws many of its metaphors from plants rather than animals. *Busu* may be such a word. According to one theory, the original meaning of *busu* is a poison derived from the root of aconite. People contort their faces and die if they ingest *busu*, a scenario that has been immortalized in Kyogen comedies. Somehow, somewhere, a connection may have been made between the grimace of a person poisoned by *busu* and a woman's ugly face. Short-lived slang variations on the ugly word have proliferated, including *seishin* (spiritual) *busu* for women whose beauty is only skin-deep, and *kamaboko* (fish sausage) *busu* for women who fit the definition of *busu* as closely as Japanese fish sausage sticks to the wooden slab on which it is prepared.

danjo Male-Female   男 女

Japan lacks a ladies-first philosophy, even in language. Male characters get the leadership positions in almost all such words as *danjo* (male-female), *fufu* (husband-wife), and *shijo* (child-girl; here "child" means "boy"). This variety of sexism even managed to infiltrate the words for sexual equality (*danjo byodo*) and sexual discrimination (*danjo sabetsu*), although a literal translation of the latter, *sei sabetsu*, is an alternative in use. Not surprisingly, some of the early Japanese travelers to reach the West were convinced that the ladies who walked first truly led the nations. Japan's traditional gentlemen-first philosophy is expressed with several phrases, which put it into practice by placing the male character ahead. These include "males respected, females despised" (*danson johi*) and "husband calls, wife follows" (*fusho fuzui*).

The term *danjo kyogaku* gives men priority at the same time that it conveys the egalitarian concept "coeducation." In a sense, this turn of phrase is accurate because boys do get preference in the Japanese school system. In the mid-1980s, almost every teacher from elementary school through high school began each school day with a class roll call listing all the boys, then all the girls. The oldest boys usually entered school ceremonies first, followed by girls of the same age, then the younger classes, also in boys-first order.

The pattern continues into adulthood. Men are practically always the first to step on and off an elevator, the first to be served at a restaurant, and the first to submerge themselves in the family bathtub each evening. Housewives used to wait for the men to finish eating before taking a bite, but times are changing. Now families like to dine simultaneously—that is, if the husband arrives home from work before the kids fall asleep. (Long work hours and mandatory drinking bouts keep many executives out so late that their families eat dinner way before they come through the door.) Another sign of progress is the way couples walk. Earlier in this century, women trailed a few steps behind their husbands. A proverb admonished them, "Three steps back, so you don't tread on the master's shadow" (*Sanpo sagatte, shi no kage o fumazu*). Regardless of shadows, nowadays women and men walk side by side.

hinoeuma no onna   Fiery-Horse Women   丙午の女

A new generation of fiery-horse women is off and galloping toward a brighter future. Until now, women (*onna*) born during the year of the "fiery horse" (*hinoeuma*) in the sixty-year cycle of the Chinese calendar have been considered dark horses unlikely to win the race to a happy life. Superstition branded females born in 1906 and 1966 as *hinoeuma*, who are as powerful as wild horses and ready to "devour" any men fool enough to marry them. *Hinoeuma* are reputed to be even more overbearing than Kate in Shakespeare's *The Taming of the Shrew*, which in Japanese is called "The Taming of the Restless Horse (*jajauma*)."

Males don't have an unlucky birth year to worry about and Japanese admit it's nonsense, but just to be on the safe side, many couples took special precautions to make sure their offspring wouldn't suffer from other people's outdated notions. The birth rate, which for a decade hovered around 18 and 19 births per thousand persons, plunged to 13.7 in 1966. The number of recorded female births drops during the dreaded year and rises in years immediately before and after. Apparently, contraception and postponed registration of birth are factors.

Although China originated this calendar based on animal totems, Chinese women do not suffer if they were born as fiery horses. The superstition was a made-in-Japan embellishment to the imported calendar. According to one theory, it originated with the Kabuki play *Yaoya Oshichi*, written in the patriarchal Edo period. It chronicles a *hinoeuma* woman whose hot temperament led her to burn down the temple where her boyfriend worked, in hopes she would get to see him more. Instead, she got burned at the stake. The story has remained in the collective consciousness of Japan ever since.

Compared to the 1906 herd, the new fiery-horse women are coming of age in greener pastures. Then marriage was virtually the only road to financial security open to women. The fiery females' reputation for destroying men put them at a disadvantage and a lot of them lived as impoverished spinsters. Modern *hinoeuma* may still have trouble finding husbands, but many count themselves lucky because they enjoy lower competition ratios for school entrance exams and job openings, due to their smaller numbers. However, some institutions have caught on to this situation. At least a few Japanese universities reduced the number of students accepted in 1985, when the *hinoeuma* came of age, so that the fiery-horse effect would not send their academic standards up in smoke. The University of Tokyo, the nation's top-ranked school, was not one of them. The competition ratio there was actually higher because so many failed applicants from prior years tried again in 1985. They figured it would be easy to gallop past the few fiery horses, who are reputed to be less disciplined academically than age groups reared under more severe competition. It remains to be seen how the fiery-horse women will fare in the marriage race, but in their educations and careers, the fiery-horse factor could be a blessing in disguise.

kashimashii Noisy   姦 し い

"Put three women together and you get noise," says a Japanese proverb. (*Onna sannin yoreba kashimashii.*) The idea is illustrated in the character *kashimashii*, which means noisy and is, predictably, comprised of the female ideogram thrice repeated. Of all the characters imported from China, it is almost always the first example that springs to mind when linguistic sex discrimination is discussed. Three women add up to a sin worse than noise when the same character is pronounced *kan*. This spells wickedness or mischief, and it can be stretched into the verb form *kansuru*, meaning to seduce, assault, or rape. The hidden corollary to the *kashimashii* character is that a trio of men getting together is nothing remarkable. There is no character composed of three male ideograms. In fact, the male symbol almost never appears as a component of other characters.

Other words reinforce the concept that women cause a hubbub. In old Japan, the most likely spot for women to gather was beside the well (*idobata*) where they drew water and washed clothes, so the term "well-side conference" (*idobata kaigi*) is still used to describe a group of gossiping women. The word for chatterbox (*oshaberi*), which literally means "honorable talker," is almost always used to describe—or put down—a woman. Gossip is considered something women do, while there are few similarly derogatory terms for men who babble about trivial topics.

ko itten   A Touch of Scarlet   紅 一 点

When a lone flower blooms brightly in the foliage, Japanese admire it for adding "a touch of scarlet" (*ko itten*). The same phrase denotes one woman in a group of men.

The linking of females with ruby hues seems commonsensical to the Japanese. Red is "pretty," an attribute females are supposed to seek. Red also means happy celebration. Tradition says it should be worn by infants and people lucky enough to hit their sixtieth birthday, because on that day they begin a new sixty-year cycle of the Chinese calendar. The undergarments worn beneath kimonos by Japanese women traditionally have been red, a color thought to ward off menstrual pain and keep the female reproductive system running smoothly. Men considered a glimpse of this red underwear to be very erotic. The few remaining kimono-clad women usually wear white underwear today, although geisha may retain the original rosy colors. The Western clothes now worn by Japanese girls are often red, until their first school days force them into more sober uniforms, usually navy blue sailor suits. School girls still choose reds for their pencil cases and other belongings, and after class they sometimes revert to rose-tinted outfits. As they grow up, most put aside their crimson wardrobes for more subdued pinks and maroons, and begin reddening their lips and cheeks with lipstick and rouge.

Ocher and vermilion paint, applied to the faces of *haniwa* clay tomb figures of the third to sixth centuries, is the earliest trace of cosmetics in Japan. Scholars say this was ritual make-up, not the true ancestor of modern-day cosmetics. Japan's first real rouge was derived from the safflower, which made its way there via China and Korea in the early seventh century. The safflower is called *benibana*, literally "scarlet flower," using an alternate pronunciation of the *ko* character in "a touch of scarlet." For more than a thousand years Japanese women used tiny brushes to paint the expensive safflower extract onto their lips. On special occasions, they reddened other parts of their faces, too. Today traditional make-up is still worn by Kabuki actors and geisha, but most Japanese women replaced their old-fashioned cosmetics with Western lipsticks and rouges around the turn of the century.

An age-old metaphor for the only male in a group of females is "a single wheat stalk in a field of mustard flowers" (*nanohana-batake ni mugi ippon*). Recently Japanese women have devised a term analogous to *ko itten*; it identifies the Japanese man, not by the color of his lips, but by the dark shade of his typical school uniform or business suit. Although the new term is less common than the original, a man in a female crowd is said to add *koku itten*, "a touch of black."

nyonin kinzei   No Females Allowed   女人禁制

Mountains, pillars of phallic symbolism in Western culture, are goddesses in the ancient Shinto pantheon. Ironically, this female imagery sometimes is used to justify the practice of "no females allowed" (*nyonin kinzei*).

Women are forbidden inside tunnels under construction because, according to the men earning a good living on tunnel-building jobs, the female mountain spirit enjoys the attentions of men so much that she would get jealous if a woman were around to distract the guys. Today's male miners figure the mountain goddess would respond to the presence of women by causing an accident. However, this did not stop mining companies from putting women to work alongside men and children in the Japanese coal mines of the late nineteenth and early twentieth centuries. Those women were rescued by protective legislation, which was in turn swept away by the Equal Employment Opportunity Law in 1986. Some women recently pointed out the silliness of *nyonin kinzei* at the Seikan Tunnel, which stretches for some thirty-three miles beneath the Tsugaru Straits, but to no avail. The world's longest undersea tunnel was completed in 1983 without one woman setting foot inside—not even Dietwoman Masako Kobayashi and other female politicians who wanted to see how tax money was being spent. Once these railway tunnels are completed, the superstition conveniently disappears and both sexes are encouraged to buy tickets to ride through the tunnel.

Not only tunnels, but also mountaintops used to be taboo to females, since high elevations were deemed holy. Mount Fuji was once considered too sacred for women to climb, though it is now open to anyone with legs strong enough to scale it. Other formerly restricted peaks are Hiei, Koya, Omine, and Ontake, all revered in Shinto or Buddhism. Women are still forbidden from "defiling" the purity of a handful of temples with their presence, but for the most part their access is much greater than before.

Similar to the mountain goddess myth are superstitions about the spirits of the sea and saké rice wine. Some young women in the 1980s still harbor girlhood memories of being denied admission to fishing boats because of the jealous sea goddess. The central saké deity is also considered a female who doesn't want to be bothered by mortal women, so breweries barred women from their wine cellars until recently.

The pristine position behind the sushi counter was once closed to women, too. In the mid-1980s, only about 15 of the 55,000 professionals who slice raw fish and slap it onto vinegared rice were female, but many male sushi chefs now scoff at the superstition that says sushi will spoil at the touch of a woman's warm, perfumed hands.

Nyonin kinzei was also enforced in the national sumo ring Kokugikan, at Kuramae, as ten-year-old Mie Kurihara found out, the hard way, in 1978. She wrestled her way to the top at local gyms as the lone girl of 276 national finalists, but she never got her shot at the championship. Officials ruled that, like all females, Mie was more "impure" than the blubbery men who usually embrace each other in the ring.

Sometimes the *nyonin kinzei* custom is applied to imported sports. The national boxing ring and baseball stadium dug-out have been off-limits to females, and a Dietwoman caused a stir in 1985 when she was denied entrance to a golf tournament involving male political leaders at one of Japan's top-class golf clubs. Mayumi Moriyama left to protest to the press, followed by some male sympathizers. Although there is no ancient Japanese superstition about golf goddesses, the club in question did defend its discriminatory policy by claiming it as a "tradition."

onna Women   女

Japanese sketch a picture of a woman every time they write the word "female." The three simple lines of *onna* evolved from a sketch of a person kneeling with hands folded, a pose seen as submissive by scholars today. *Onna* is easy enough to be one of the initial characters taught to Japanese first-graders, who usually don't study the more complicated character for "male" (*otoko*) until the following year. Japanese dictionaries explain that rice paddies are where men must exert their strength through farming, so "male" is conveyed by putting a paddy (a square with a cross inside) above power (a sketch of a muscular arm). Characters unite sign and symbol, so the three strokes that signify the sound *onna* are also used symbolically in the same way that Westerners indicate "female" by drawing a circle balanced on a cross, a sign developed in medieval times to resemble the mirror of the goddess Venus. Each symbol is popular with the women's liberation movement of its own culture.

For *onna*, this is the start of a renaissance. Like English-speaking feminists who insist they are not ladies but women, Japanese feminists began to use the word during the 1960s to describe themselves. Both *onna* and *otoko* are informal and crude, and emphasize sexuality. When someone "becomes a woman" (*onna ni naru*), it frequently means she has lost her virginity. However, these words do put people a step above animals, which have their own terms for female (*mesu*) and male (*osu*). The plain *onna* and *otoko* are often used to insult, the way an English speaker might berate an "ill-tempered female" or an "egocentric male." In more dignified conversation, these ruffians are combined with the character for "gender," creating the words *josei* (lady) and *dansei* (gentleman). To be even more flattering, a character composed of the female ideogram holding a duster is often followed by "person" to create *fujin*, a classy-looking word for women used in government documents and department store ads.

A newly popular field of scholarly research looks at how the *onna* ideogram is used to build other characters. *Otoko* is rarely used for character-building, but the female symbol is mated with sundry other signs to become an accomplice in a myriad of characters, many with negative implications.

A female and an eyebrow means flattery (*kobi*), while female and disease comprise a verb (*sonemu*) meaning to be jealous. A woman between two men means to tease (*naburu*); this is used in a compound with "murder" to say "death by torture" (*naburi-goroshi*). The *onna* symbol thrice repeated (*kashimashii*) means noisy or evil. A woman and a hand—that is, a seized woman—means a servant (*do*). A heart written below this character for servant makes the verb for becoming angry (*okoru*).

Other characters, while not negative per se, reveal assumptions about gender roles. "Woman" and "few" add up to "exquisite" (*taenaru*) because a woman of few years is considered so. Pleasure (*go*) is indicated by a combination of "woman" with the verb for receiving from an inferior. A good female always means daughter (*musume*). To wed is illustrated by "woman" and "take" (*metoru*). A woman is thought to marry into her husband's house, so "woman" plus "house" conveys bride or daughter-in-law (*yome*). A woman under a roof means being contented (*yasumaru*). Motherhood is exalted—and fatherhood ignored—in what is probably the most common woman-based character, *suki*. It conveys fondness, goodwill, and desirability by putting a child with a woman. These characters were imported centuries ago from China, and many are still included in the list of roughly two thousand general-use characters that every student is taught before graduation from high school. Of those described, about half are on the list: *do*, *okoru*, *taenaru*, *musume*, *yome*, *yasumaru*, *go*, and *suki*.

Among the few characters built around the male (*otoko*) symbol are "nephew" (*oi*), which joins "male" with "life," and "father-in-law" (*shuto*), which links it with "mortar." Neither is a general-use character, but two characters designated for common usage *seem* to include the masculine sign. This pair, "courageous" (*isamashii*) and "captive or slave" (*ryo*), actually include more complex ideograms that have been simplified to look like "man."

onna moji   Female Lettering   女 文 字

The sexes used to write differently in Japan. Women wrote phonetically while men expressed themselves with thousands of ideograms imported from China. The set of cursive phonetic symbols for syllables used to be called "female lettering" (*onna moji* or *onna-gana*) or "female hand" (*onna-de*). The roughly fifty symbols still in use are best known today as *hiragana*, literally "common, ordinary syllabary." They are much easier to learn than the Chinese characters once called "male lettering" (*otoko moji*) or "male hand" (*otoko-de*). Mastering the elaborate system of characters requires an extensive education, an experience available only to a male elite in the days of *onna moji*.

Japanese existed solely as a spoken language until about the sixth century, when the first attempts were made to force Japanese speech into the elaborate writing system devised by and for the Chinese. The fit was clumsy. While the elite struggled with this impossible task, the common people, both female and male, broke down the Chinese ideograms into a more usable phonetic form. Thus, the "female lettering" developed by around the tenth century owes its existence partially to female ingenuity.

Japanese writing today mixes Chinese characters with *hiragana* and *katakana*, another phonetic alphabet which is reserved primarily for foreign words. However, the nation's first great literary works were written by women and therefore in "female lettering." Best known is *The Tale of Genji*, reputed to be the world's first novel, written by Murasaki Shikibu in the eleventh century.

Nowadays when children start school, the first letters they learn are the gentle lines of the old "female lettering," but an adult writer who used only *hiragana* would be considered uneducated at best. "Female lettering" does not command respect, while the more Chinese characters one knows, the more she or he will be esteemed as a learned person. Words composed solely of these ideograms carry prestige even when spoken, rather like Latinate words in English. An example is the unpretentious *taberu* (to eat) versus *shokuji o suru* (to dine). The gender-based division of written Japanese also lingers in the calligraphy world, where women tend to concentrate on the flowing strokes of female lettering while men perfect their Chinese characters.

onna-rashisa Femininity 女らしさ

One way to chart the meaning of femininity (*onna-rashisa*) in Japan is to listen to how the landscape itself is described. A "male hill" (*otoko-zaka*) is the steeper side of a hill, while the more gently sloping grade is termed the "female hill" (*onna-zaka*). This seldom-used phrase was resurrected by author Fumiko Enchi as the title for her novel about a wife who waits decades to get revenge for her husband's infidelity, though the English translation of *Onna-zaka* is titled simply *The Waiting Years*. Another way of using nature to summarize the character of the sexes is the proverb "Men are pine trees, women are wisteria vines" (*Otoko wa matsu, onna wa fuji*), which means men are the strong base to which women cling.

The positive traits associated with women are bundled up and tied together in the word *onna-rashisa*. Dictionaries define it in terms of being kind, gentle, polite, submissive, and graceful. Sometimes "weak" is included, spurring feminist scholars to protest in the 1980s. Many people would also add cheerfulness to the list of what gives a woman *onna-rashisa*.

On the other hand, the Japanese have several insults based on the linking of women with certain character faults. "Rotten as a woman" is an insult hurled at Japanese men by accusers of both sexes. *Onna no kusatta yo na* is a standard reproach for guys whom Westerners might call wimps or sissies. These fellows may also be assaulted with a negative word built from two "woman" ideograms, *memeshii* (effeminate). Both men and women are offended when someone denounces them as "womanish" (*josei-teki*). The trait that often shakes loose this avalanche of abuse is mealy-mouthed indecisiveness. Sometimes the criticism is cloaked in poetic imagery. "A woman's heart and the autumn sky" (*Onna-*

gokoro to aki no sora), croons a proverb. The connection is that fall weather in Japan shifts quickly, just as the moods of a woman's heart. The word *onna-gokoro* is usually used in the context of love, where such fickleness is generally unwelcome.

otoko masari Male-Surpassers   男 勝 り

An *otoko masari* is a woman who excels over men in some way. She has more brains or muscles or just plain spirit. One of the most famous *otoko masari* is the late-tenth-century author Sei Shonagon, who blended diary, essay, and fiction into *The Pillow Book*, a Japanese literary classic. Positive though its definition sounds, *otoko masari* is not a type Japanese girls aspire to become. The word, literally meaning "male-surpasser," is a put-down. For example, there is much grumbling in the halls of Japan's coed colleges these days about *otoko masari* types who take their studies seriously and plan to compete against their male classmates on the job market as well. It implies not only extra ability, but also lack of femininity.

The female upstart is likely to begin life as an *otenba*, what an English speaker calls a tomboy. *Otenba*, literally "honorable twisting and turning granny," suggests health and energy. People often use it to describe their own rambunctious offspring. A Japanese girl can get away with being a tomboy until about age twenty, but then tradition calls for her to settle down and avoid challenging the males around her.

If she doesn't, she is denounced as an *otoko masari* or another taunt drawn from the large body of Japanese words in which the sexes battle for superiority. She is said to achieve "in spite of being a woman" (*onna-datera ni* or *onna no kuse ni*). She brings about "male loss of face" (*otoko kaomake*) because she is "more than a man" (*otoko ijo*). Men are the measure for most types of accomplishment, but in the realm of sewing, cooking, or child rearing, guys can cause "female loss of face" (*onna kaomake*) when their prowess makes them "more than a woman" (*onna ijo*). Women also are the standard for inferiority; one way to show contempt for a man is to call him "less than a woman" (*onna ika*). Females being inferior to males has been considered so unremarkable that no parallel expression exists. Likewise, there is only one way to say "in spite of being a man" (*otoko no kuse ni*) and no such thing as a "female-surpasser."

otoko yaku   Male Impersonators   男役

The romantic fantasies of many Japanese girls focus on love affairs with dashingly handsome women dressed as men. These "male roles" (*otoko yaku*) are the superstars of the four-hundred-member Takarazuka Grand Theater troupe, the twentieth-century female counterpart of the historic Kabuki theater. The Takarazuka actresses stage about seven performances a week at both of their three-thousand-seat theaters for almost entirely female audiences.

Kabuki, revered as one of Japan's three major classical theater forms, was actually originated by a woman named Okuni, a female attendant at Izumo Shrine. Tradition says that she led a band of mostly female performers in a dance and comedy show on a dry riverbed in Kyoto in 1603. The crowd loved it and the style spread nationwide. The creators of Kabuki soon became victims of their own popularity because onlookers tended to fight over the actresses, who also performed acts of prostitution on the side. To cool the unruliness, the Tokugawa shogunate banned all female entertainers from Kabuki in 1629. This and subsequent edicts toned down the exuberant new entertainment into the slow-paced, highly stylized art that it is now.

Men were quick to fill in the gender gap, and in the late seventeenth century the female impersonator began to be called "female form," two characters pronounced either *oyama* or *onnagata*. The impersonators literally lived their role, maintaining dressing rooms separate from the actors who played men and continuing to dress, speak, and move like women in their private lives as well. Today top *oyama* enjoy equal status with their counterparts who portray men. Theater lovers of both genders flock to Kabuki shows, where they tend to admire these *oyama* for their artistic skill in projecting femininity. Their reputation as weaklings and homosexuals, however, dampens some people's enthusiasm.

The extreme stylization of Kabuki is sometimes mentioned as an excuse for men to continue monopolizing all roles in the best Kabuki theaters, long after the shogun's other decrees have been forgotten. The *oyama* are not trying to be real women, but to be female impersonators, a role that comes more naturally to men, or so the argument goes. Nowadays women do perform in amateur and lesser known Kabuki theaters, even to the point of impersonating men.

While Japanese theater has a long tradition of single-sex casting, contemporary comic books aimed at Japanese girls have gone a step further to serialize romances between beautiful, sensitive gay men, who are called "honorable pots" (*okama*) in slang. From this came an unflattering vogue word for girls who search for real-life versions of their comic-book darlings by attaching themselves to gay men. Japanese speculate that they are attracted by the safety of being with gays, or by a common interest in fashion, or simply because they can't catch a boyfriend. Their close association with the "pots" brands them as *okoge*, a term usually applied to burned rice stuck to the bottom of a pot.

Takarazuka provides a modern version of the colorful Kabuki performances. With Broadway songs on their lips and sequins all over their costumes, Takarazuka actresses mix kick lines and a disco beat with foreign stories such as *The Arabian Nights* or the pilgrims' discovery of America. Sometimes they reach into Japanese folklore for a plot, but the result is always a gaudy, glittery love story, as it has been since the troupe's founding in 1914. The dazzling spectacles staged by Takarazuka are sponsored by a thoroughly conservative corporation whose other interests include nothing more risqué than railroads and department stores. Most adults laugh indulgently at the packs of teenage girls waiting breathlessly at the stage door for the moment when they can see, take photographs of, beg autographs from, give presents to, and maybe even touch their favorite male impersonator.

ryote ni hana   Flowers in Both Hands 両手に花

Flowery language is used to describe Japanese women starting when they are still just "buds" (*tsubomi*), a synonym for virgins. One of the instances when English speakers use such imagery is in talking about how men "deflower" virgins, but when Japanese women lose their virginity, the floral imagery bursts into full blossom.

A man seated between two women is said to have "flowers in both hands" (*ryote ni hana*). Originally, it simply meant "doubly blessed" and was applied to men with both learning and talent, or any two valuable possessions. Especially comely women are praised with this proverb: "If she stands, a Chinese peony. If she sits, a tree peony. And her walking form, a lily." (*Tateba shaku-yaku, suwareba botan, aruku sugata wa yuri no hana.*) Peonies of all sorts are renowned in Japan for their eye-catching beauty and bright colors. Lilies, on the other hand, suggest a modest demeanor and lithe figure. When she retained her good looks past her prime, a woman used to be called a "late-blooming cherry blossom" (*uba-zakura*). The woman who fits the traditional ideal by humbly anticipating and fulfilling the needs of men is complimented as a "Japanese pink" (*Yamato nadeshiko*). Yet if she is too shy at a party, she may become one of the ignored "wallflowers" (*kabe no hana*) who hesitates near the wall while others enjoy themselves. Women who work are often called "office flowers" (*shokuba no hana*). Or, surrounded by darkly dressed male executives, they are likened to a lone red posy that adds a charming "touch of red" (*ko itten*) to an otherwise plain field. Many females are adorned with names containing floral characters, such as Hanako, literally "flower child," while names based on birth order traditionally go to males.

A teenage girl training to become a geisha is called a "new flower" (*shinbana*) for about the first year after her debut. This is just the start of the floral images that flourish in the world of geishas and prostitutes, whose pleasure quarters were termed "flower towns" (*hanamachi*). For their services, men paid "flower fees" (*hanadai*). This whole subculture used to be referred to as the "flower-and-willow world" (*karyukai*). Neither herbal image referred to the men who bought pleasure. The willowy geisha specialized in artistic performances while the courtesans were considered "flowers" who offered garden-variety sexual favors. However, both genders were susceptible to "flower-and-willow sickness" (*karyubyo*), better known in English as venereal disease.

2

Christmas Cake Sweepstakes
GIRLHOOD TO WEDDING

boku   Me, the Tough Guy   僕

Little girls in Japan quickly learn they should not match an "I" for an "I" with little boys. Preschoolers of either gender commonly refer to themselves by their given name followed by a diminutive akin to "dear" (-*chan*), but about the time that they start school, girls begin calling themselves *atashi* while boys choose the alternative *boku*. Literally "manservant," the exclusively masculine *boku* is the informal "I" preferred by boys and men. However, for the past twenty years at least, a minority of Japanese females between the ages of twelve and twenty-five has been referring to themselves with the boyish *boku*. Some are trying to be cute, others are just contrary. In the 1980s, the trend began to be reinforced by comic books and novels in which the heroines call themselves *boku*.

Speaking Japanese would seem to provoke an identity crisis, for there are many different words for "I." To pick one is to identify oneself by gender, age, and level of respect felt toward the listener. Those used primarily by females include *atashi*, *atakushi*, and *atai*, while men generally say *boku*, *ore*, and *washi*. Both genders call themselves *watakushi* in such cases as answering phones, giving speeches, and talking to superiors or strangers. Both can also use its informal abbreviation *watashi*. The choice of an "I" is one of the hallmarks differentiating feminine language (*onna kotoba*) from the neutral and masculine ways of speaking Japanese. Women's speech differs in vocabulary, intonation, and its more frequent use of polite forms and gentle-sounding particles at the ends of sentences.

The *boku* girls are just one example of how this rigid system is breaking down. Girls have also been scandalizing the nation in the 1970s and 1980s by adopting other aspects of their male classmates' rough speech style. The Japanese have developed diverse explanations for the phenomenon. Perhaps the girls think it's fun to ignore the rules of genteel speaking. Could it be, some observers wonder, that their parents neglected to teach them how to speak properly? Maybe they subconsciously wish to be male. Or their motive could be to use *boku* to communicate casually as peers with boys, who show no desire to soften their tough-guy talk. On territory traditionally considered male, such as a university engineering class, both sexes sometimes refer to themselves as *boku*. This usage supports the theory that the important distinction in Japanese speech is not feminine/masculine, but private/public or conciliatory/assertive.

burikko   The Pretenders   ぶりっ子

To attract boyfriends, American girls pretend they are women, while Japanese women pretend they are girls. American girls, who grow up toying with busty Barbie dolls, usually can't wait to start dressing themselves in bras, make-up, and high heels. In contrast, the Japanese ideal is a naive teenager, so women tend to play dumb for years after giving up their virginity. These falsely cute types are called *burikko*, or "pretending kids."

An example of the ultimate *burikko* is Seiko Matsuda, Japan's most popular female singer of the 1980s. Flat-chested and bow-legged, she sells about three million singles and one million LPs annually. By 1985, at the grand old age of twenty-two, she had sold 30 billion yen ($200 million) in records and tapes. Pop music idols start young in Japan, usually making their debut at age fifteen in what promoters openly admit is an effort to appeal to Japanese men's "Lolita complex" (*Rori-kon*). Not only singers, but also many movie stars and models strive for Matsuda's cutie-pie look. Japanese seem to be drawn to media images of females who appear as approachable as the girl next door. The word *burikko* was coined by one of these young "talents," Kuniko Yamada, on a television program in 1980.

"Cutie" (*kawaiko-chan*) is another term for the imitation innocents who are so common in Japan that a rich vocabulary exists to name them. Another synonym supposedly comes from the way such a woman feigns ignorance. She is likely to look at a *kamaboko* (a fish-paste sausage mounted on a wooden slab) and ask something silly like, "Is *kamaboko* a kind of fish (*toto* in baby talk) that has wood on its belly?" Hence, the word *kamatoto*.

Against this background, it's not surprising that Japan is the only country where Barbie dolls did not sell when they were first introduced. That is, Barbie didn't sell well until toy makers redesigned her into a cute pretender who appears less buxom, less glamorous, shorter, and younger.

In pre-industrial Japan, dating did not exist in word or in deed. Marriage introductions (*miai*) served one of the purposes that dating does in the West. People still joke about wimps who are so busy cramming as students and working overtime as employees that the closest they ever come to dating is a marriage introduction. On the other hand, the Japanese of old could engage in escapades such as the "intimacy pull" (*aibiki*), a term used when sweethearts met on the sly. The idea that a female and male can decide on their own to get together without concealing their plans is so alien to Japanese tradition that a foreign term had to be borrowed: *deeto o suru* (to do a date).

According to a survey by Sanwa Bank, more than one out of five couples who married in Japan in 1984 met through formal introductions. Each year the ratio of "love marriages" (*renai kekkon*) inches higher, while the arranged marriage (*miai kekkon*) procedure has grown so casual that some couples have trouble defining which type of match they made. A hundred years ago, the couple wasn't even allowed to speak during the *miai*. The fathers did all the talking. Some maidens were too polite and shy to lift their eyes from the tatami-mat floor, so it was really the bachelors who got a good look. Even after it was over, the couple had little say about whether they would wed. Marriage was a family matter decided by the patriarchs on both sides.

Today's lovers don't necessarily bring their parents along anymore. A modern *miai* can be an offhand introduction of two friends at a baseball game. Among the most common trysting spots are the lobbies of first-class hotels, from which the couple proceeds to a coffee shop to chat. This updated system allows them to evaluate each other's character once questions of income and health have been settled by go-betweens. After revealing their hobbies and goals, and taking a hard look at the prospects, Japanese today decide for themselves whom to marry. Men usually settle for one of the first potential mates they meet, while some choosy women go through as many as thirty *miai*.

Japanese who use the arranged marriage system do not bid farewell to the prospect of love. They hope love will unfold gradually as they get to know each other. They view *miai* as not only an easy way to find a mate, but also a safe way, because relying on a matchmaker eliminates encounters with people from different backgrounds likely to cause tragic clashes. In the words of a spokesman for a computerized matchmaking service, "This method prevents a situation like Romeo and Juliet's."

Whether their relationship is introduced or self-induced, it is the boy who is supposed to ask the girl out on subsequent dates. Typically he will suggest they go to a movie or a coffee shop. Other popular dates include picnicking, sightseeing, shopping, taking a drive, or going to a restaurant, concert, or disco. A boy also can hang out at a coffee shop or disco and pick up a girl for casual sex. The Japanese expression for this is "to play the softy" (*nanpa suru*), as opposed to the "toughy" (*koha*) who is too busy with martial arts to care about girls. The passive role is played by girls, who say they "are softied" (*nanpa sareru*).

Women do take the initiative in a smaller way every year on Valentine's Day, February 14, when Japanese females from grade school on up assert their affection by giving chocolates to the men in their lives. No red-blooded Japanese male would consider presenting his ladylove with valentine goodies. Western valentine roles were turned topsy-turvy by Japanese confectionery companies, which introduced the custom in the 1960s to boost chocolate sales. The plan worked so well that 1986 valentine candy sales hit 40 billion yen ($266 million). Many gifts are the "obligatory chocolate" (*giri-choko*) that female workers feel compelled to bestow upon their male bosses and coworkers. Roving saleswomen, such as those who peddle insurance, have adopted valentine chocolates as a sales tool to reward customers of both sexes. Attempts to make Japanese men return the favor seem to go against the grain. Candy makers have met little success in their campaign to convince boys and men to shower their beloved with white chocolate, marshmallows, and cookies on March 14, which they've christened White Day (*howaito dee*).

hako-iri musume   Daughters-in-a-Box   箱入り娘

Precious dolls, scrolls, and tea bowls should be stored in wooden boxes to protect them from the hazardous world. Japanese see a parallel between caring for their treasured possessions and for a daughter. They express it with the phrase *hako-iri musume*, which translates literally as "daughter-in-a-box" and means sheltered maiden. Most people still consider the phrase a compliment that suggests the loving protection with which parents rear their girls. However, the boxed daughter is beginning to acquire a negative image as a painfully shy girl who doesn't know how to do anything besides sit prettily within the confines of a boxlike Japanese home and value system. A male version of the term does not exist.

The power of the daughter-in-a-box concept was demonstrated dramatically by an incident that occurred in 1883. Toshiko Kishida, Japan's first female journalist, was inspired to eloquence in a speech against the cramping of female freedom. "*Hako-iri musume*, in my definition, are those girls who cannot act, cannot talk, cannot even move their hands and feet, as if they were trapped in a box," she said. "Their parents may say, 'Well, we're not doing this to limit her freedom, but to give her a good moral education and because we love her.' However, they don't realize their actions do end up limiting her freedom and causing her pain." Roused to defensive fury, the local police in the Kyoto suburb where she was speaking arrested her for "dangerous, left-wing" agitation and fined her the equivalent of a month's salary.

Today many Japanese women work outside the home before they marry, but employers perpetuate the boxed-in mentality by making sure that, if they hire an unmarried woman, she still lives with her family. Safeguarding her innocence is only part of the motive. Companies can pay the stay-at-homes less. They can also demand more because mothers are available to cook and clean for daughters worn out on the job.

One of the perils lurking outside the box is knowledge of sex. If this topic reaches a girl's ears, she may be belittled as an "ear-biddy" (*mimi-doshima*) who has been aged not by action, but by hearing. The slur also suggests she may boast as if she herself were sexually experienced. Becoming elderly by ear is an affliction Japanese boys simply are never accused of contracting, though the written characters themselves bear no gender. *Mimi* means ear and *toshima* refers not very nicely to middle-aged women.

Hako-iri musume have been raised in an impregnable environment, but that doesn't mean they aren't curious about life beyond the box. "A bug spoiled the daughter-in-a-box" (*Hako-iri musume ni mushi ga tsuita*) is how observers criticize the advances made by an undesirable guy. Originally, the pesky bugs were all male, but now the phrase can also be applied to men whose lives have been infested by unwelcome women.

hanayome shugyo Bridal Training   花嫁修業

The slow-motion ritual of the tea ceremony and the art of arranging flowers to look more spontaneous than nature itself are considered part of "bridal training" (*hanayome shugyo*) in Japan. By age twenty, many women have begun to ready themselves for marriage by learning these esoteric arts, both dating back to the sixteenth century. Some observers credit this custom with preserving cultural traditions that would otherwise fall by the wayside in today's pragmatic world. Ironically, women were banned from practicing tea ceremony when it was first invented. Nowadays men rarely study tea or flowers, but male influence lives on in the term for pupils of these arts. They are all called "younger brothers" (*deshi*).

Although a 1986 survey by the newspaper *Nikkei Ryutsu Shinbun* showed flower arrangement was the most common form of bridal training, many girls seek more with-it ways to develop themselves. Cooking topped the survey's list of subjects girls want to study. Second-ranked English conversation beat out both flower arrangement and tea ceremony, which still spark more enthusiasm than aerobic exercise. Japanese sometimes characterize the modern girl's idea of bridal training as a trio of up-to-date subjects: English conversation, word processing, and driver's education.

The seemingly frivolous tea and flower lessons have applications in wedded life, though perhaps not immediately apparent. The key to understanding lies in the word *shugyo*, which means training through discipline and ascetic rigors, such as those endured by Buddhist monks. Thus, *hanayome shugyo* is more than the piano playing and other womanly refinements historically cultivated by European ladies to fulfill their role as entertainers. By studying these painstaking arts, Japanese women develop the patience and introspection considered essential to contentment as a wife. The fact that a woman or her family can afford to pay for her lessons is also said to make her even more marriageable.

Becoming a "housework helper" (*kaji tetsudai*) can be another way to train to be a bride. A woman who identifies herself as a *kaji tetsudai*—whether in conversation or on an official document—does not work as a hired maid; if she did, she would be called "honorable helper" (*otetsudai-san*). The humble housework helper makes herself useful around her parents' home in the interval after completing her education and before marrying. If she never weds, she can retain this position for life. Highly educated young women spend days, months, and even years at home with full family approval, partly because many parents believe it is the best training for becoming a full-time housewife. Not every family can afford to support a *kaji tetsudai*, so the term summons up images of wealth, and fashion magazines feature the designer wardrobes of these homebodies. However, the custom of staying home as a housework helper is disappearing as more young women enter the labor force.

For women of all income levels, home used to be the setting for lessons in the practical arts of cooking and cleaning, as well as any instruction in flowers and tea, but nowadays few girls grow up helping their moms with housework. Both genders are pampered at least through high school so they can concentrate on studying. Sooner or later, parents usually pay for their daughters to receive bridal training outside the home. Culture centers, private schools and even hotels teach brides-to-be, as do female neighbors licensed in the traditional arts. Home tutoring is one way that traditional Japanese arts can prove as practical as a modern bridal training course in word processing. Many women earn incomes, sometimes substantial ones, by teaching everything from flower arranging to English and piano to the new generation eager for bridal training.

hina matsuri   Doll Festival   雛 祭

Both Girls' Day and Children's Day are celebrated in Japan. Ancient festivals developed fair and square with Girls' Day on March 3 and Boys' Day on May 5, but in 1948 reformers decided to consolidate them into one celebration for kids by elevating

Boys' Day into a national holiday for both genders. However, tradition isn't changed so easily. Families still follow the old Boys' Day customs on the date designated as Children's Day, and Girls' Day continues to be observed despite its lack of status as an official holiday.

In Japanese, Girls' Day is most commonly called *hina matsuri*, literally "Doll Festival," though it goes by such other names as *onna no sekku* (Girls' Day). Modern mothers seem to get even more pleasure than their daughters from the Girls' Day tradition of setting up a display of dolls (*hina*) representing the emperor, empress, and court attendants, all in ancient dress. Together the young and the young-at-heart admire these miniature royalty over pink-and-green rice cakes washed down with weak, sweet saké. The dolls, which are displayed for about a week before the festival, can range from a simple pair created by folding paper origami-style to an expensive five- or seven-tiered display of figures with painted clay faces and brocade kimonos. The imperial couple sits on the top level, while on the descending steps range ladies-in-waiting, court musicians, guardians, footmen, imperial household goods, and all the accouterments of a miniature bridal trousseau. The dolls and their accessories are supposed to remain with a girl throughout her lifetime, sometimes becoming valuable family heirlooms passed on to the next generation.

There was nothing pretentious about the dolls at the ancient rites that foreshadowed today's Doll Festival. The roots of the holiday stretch back more than a millennium to a Chinese purification ceremony held in the third lunar month on the day of the snake, a potent protector who rules both fertility and death. On that day, people fashioned dolls from paper, and embellished them with their own names and ages. They went to a river or beach to float away their surrogate and, they hoped, any threatening bad luck.

In addition to their ability to exorcise ill fortune, dolls had a strong power to amuse children. Little princesses of the Heian period apparently were the first to call them "chicks" (*hiina*), possibly because their dolls were as small and cute as baby birds. It was not until the Edo period that all of these traditions evolved into a holiday resembling contemporary celebrations. Imperial edicts regulating the size of the *hina* dolls suggest that parents then, as now, were eager to pamper their daughters on that day.

No amount of merrymaking, however, drives out concerns about the girls' marriage prospects. In days gone by, the holiday soup made from clams provided the pieces for a matrimonial shell game. The traditional Girls' Day pastime of matching each half shell with its mate was a way of teaching girls to be faithful to their future husbands. Even now, the dolls are whisked back into the closet immediately following the holiday. Superstition says that the longer the dolls remain out after March 3, the longer it will take for the daughter of the house to land a husband.

joshidaisei Coeds   女子大生

Japanese female university students (*joshidaisei*) major in fashion and fun, according to the popular myths building up around these relatively new and unusual folks. With a few exceptions, there were no such creatures enrolled in universities until coeducation became law in 1947. Before that, the sexes were divided from middle school onward, with boys flowing through universities while girls were diverted to women's normal schools. *Joshidaisei* is an abbreviation of the generic term for university student, prefaced by a common word for young women (*joshi*). It is applied to those who attend either the new all-women universities or the venerable institutions that are now coeducational. Creating an equivalent with the male prefix (*danshi*) simply provokes laughter with its redundancy.

The women who entered these bastions of knowledge on the heels of the postwar education reforms were serious scholars. Then, starting in the mid-1950s, a university diploma began to be viewed as a passport to employment. Today's *joshidaisei* have made a hairpin turn; many attend university to avoid or at least postpone taking a full-time job. Instead of burying themselves in books, they have a reputation as airheads who further their "education" with ski trips, sightseeing, and designer fashions. These luxuries cost money, which is said to be another mark of the *joshidaisei*. Virtually all of them are supported by their parents, and many do part-time work to supplement the allowance they get from home. The typical Japanese guy, too, relies on his family to pay for his university education, which both sexes tend to regard as a four-year vacation earned by passing the rigorous entrance exams. Despite these similar attributes, male students do not attract as much curious speculation as their female classmates.

The Japanese media have pounced on the *joshidaisei* and portrayed her as a sex kitten, much like the media-created coed of American pop culture in the 1960s. For example, in the mid-1980s it was common for young, amateur *joshidaisei* to assist anchor men on late-night television shows covering sex for male viewers. The erotic image is not totally without basis. Some *joshidaisei* do pose nude for peep shows or prostitute themselves to earn extra spending money. However, a 1986 government study showed that only four percent of women investigated for prostitution were students.

When the fun is over and their diplomas are in hand, *joshidaisei* face dim job prospects. Higher education slightly raises the employment ratio for men, but it is still a handicap for Japanese women. A 1981 government survey revealed that about seventy percent of Japanese firms did not hire female university graduates at all. Women who graduate from two-year colleges are more likely to get jobs because, in contrast to university grads, they accept lower pay and more menial work, they are younger, and the companies aren't legally bound to promote, train, or pay them on a par with the male employees. Many bosses figure women with university degrees will not work as many years as those hired at younger ages, since they expect all females to retire upon marriage.

---

ojosama   Debutantes   お 嬢 様

In a nation that considers itself solidly middle class, people call each other's daughters *ojosan*, a word with the aristocratic nuance of "young ladies." When the suffix is replaced by *-sama*, the term takes on layers of refinement like a princess putting on petticoats. No amount of yen can make a Japanese girl into an *ojosama*. This word denotes girls born and raised in "good families," which means noble blood or top executive status at a large business. *Ojosama* implies high class and good breeding, like the English word "debutante." In overwhelmingly bourgeois Japan, fascination with these rare and rarefied young ladies swelled into an "*ojosama* boom" in the mid-1980s.

Magazines for teenage boys were full of schemes on how to approach an *ojosama*, while girls' magazines gushed with articles such as "From Now On, *You Too*, Are an *Ojosama*!!" The recipe for whipping up an *ojosama* out of an ordinary girl called for large measures of neatness, reserve, and classic fashions. An *ojosama* wears color-coordinated dresses of basic design to give an overall impression of orthodoxy. But the true mark of an *ojosama*, the one the magazines gloss over because girls cannot purchase or will it, is an upbringing that leaves intact her innocence and modesty. An *ojosama* is intelligent, yet devoid of street smarts.

Her naiveté may be nurtured further at an *ojosama gakko*, or "young ladies' school." The implication is that these four-year women's colleges are like Western finishing schools, where debutantes receive polish before marrying. Some students at these institutions are far from finished with serious study and just as eager for careers as their counterparts at coed universities. They seem to have more trouble landing good jobs, however, partly because their alma maters lack academic prestige and perhaps also because of the *ojosama*'s notoriety for unworldliness.

The Japanese themselves wonder why *ojosama* suddenly captured the middle-class imagination. Some theorize that increasing independence for women has made both sexes idealize the "good old days" when even females who were not *ojosama* had more reserve. Others figure prosperity is the cause: Now that almost all Japanese have enough wealth to believe they are middle class, people want to set themselves apart with valuables that cannot be purchased, such as the *ojosama*'s innocent aura.

ryosai kenbo   Good Wives and Wise Mothers   良妻賢母

Some of Japan's best high schools and colleges for women share the same motto. *Ryosai kenbo*, the brave new slogan chosen by these pioneers in education for females, means "good wives and wise mothers." This was the primary aim of Japanese women's schools back in the late nineteenth century when they first opened their doors, and its influence lingers to this day.

The phrase "good wives and wise mothers" has long been a focal point for discussion of what girls should be taught. Masanao Nakamura coined it in his 1875 essay in the journal *Meiroku Zasshi*. He presented the classic Western model of ideal womanhood, which he must have observed during his previous travels in Europe. Women are naturally endowed with a strong moral and religious sense, he argued, and thus they are more qualified for child rearing than their husbands. He also advocated equal education for girls and boys. For those times, such suggestions were revolutionary because all official authority over children's upbringing was in the hands of their fathers and older brothers. From this hopeful start, *ryosai kenbo* was soon reshaped into a pillar supporting the Confucian-based male hierarchy. In 1899, the Japanese government instituted regulations requiring each prefecture to support at least one high school for women with a standardized curriculum to mold "good wives and wise mothers" by narrowly educating them in practical child-care skills.

Subsequent reforms have made the curricula for boys and girls almost identical. A government advisory committee was formed in the mid-1980s to examine the differences that remain, especially the guideline that said all high school girls should take four units (140 classes of fifty minutes each) of home economics while boys were building strength and competitive spirit in physical education class.

Girls are now as likely as boys to continue past the nine years of compulsory education by tackling high school. However, something akin to the *ryosai kenbo* mentality seems to restrain women from studying subjects considered "masculine." After high school, most women who decide to stay in school enter two-year colleges to absorb practical knowledge such as secretarial skills. Unlike the American junior college system, Japan's two-year college system does not enable graduates to enter midstream into four-year institutions. Meanwhile, almost all men continuing their education go to four-year colleges and universities. Even those women who do vault into university tend to make a soft landing with majors considered appropriate for women, such as humanities and education. In 1983, only two percent dared to try engineering, the field chosen by a quarter of the men.

Though most Japanese women major in "feminine" subjects,

women's studies (*joseigaku*) courses are still so new that the word is unfamiliar to older Japanese. The number of college courses on women's studies offered nationwide has grown from nineteen in the late 1970s to ninety-four in 1984, according to a study by the National Women's Education Center. Taught mostly by female teachers, the subject appeals to both genders. The same study found that slightly over half of the students enrolled in women's studies classes were male.

seijin no hi   Coming-of-Age Day   成人の日

Young women are likely to choose January 15 to pose for portraits that will be shown to potential marriage partners. The date is convenient because many women who turn twenty in that year dress up in their fanciest kimonos anyway to celebrate Coming-of-Age Day (*seijin no hi*). Twenty is the age of legal majority in Japan, so every Japanese town honors them with a simple ceremony, perhaps a speech from the mayor at a public assembly hall. Afterward, women like to find a scenic shrine or temple to set off their kimonos for the camera. The civic ceremony makes boys into men, too. However, contemporary males rarely wear kimonos no matter what their age, so they don't necessarily pose formally on that day. Preparing for marriage is also appropriate on Coming-of-Age Day because many Japanese believe people do not reach full adulthood until they wed.

January 15 was a holiday with a very different meaning for centuries before it was renamed and designated a national holiday in 1948. It used to be Women's New Year (*onna shogatsu*), also called Little New Year (*ko-shogatsu*). On this one day of the year, women were given a break from cooking and cleaning, tasks that reach a crescendo during the "big" New Year's festivities around January 1, Japan's major holiday. Not much seems to have happened on Women's New Year, except the eating of simple food, the greeting of friends, and the burning of New Year's decorations.

During those bygone days, girls marked their passage to womanhood more elaborately than in the modern Coming-of-Age Day. For example, in some areas custom decreed that girls who reached a set age should make pilgrimages to mountaintops. Once they had become adults, they signaled their status to the world by switching to grown-up hairstyles, headgear, footwear, and other accessories.

Until the twelfth century, girls also indicated their coming-of-age by tooth blackening (*ohaguro*). A stain was made by soaking scraps of iron in a concoction of tea, saké, and/or vinegar. This mixture was then painted onto the teeth every day or so. The stain was thought to protect teeth and augment beauty, since teeth were considered a repulsively exposed part of the skeleton. Gradually the custom spread to men of the nobility and warrior classes, but by the eighteenth century it was strictly a feminine practice, this time employed by all married women to announce their wedded status. Tooth blackening was prohibited as part of a national modernization program in 1868 after the arrival of wedding-ringed Westerners who expressed revulsion at the Japanese indicator of marriage and majority.

sukeban　Boss Girls　　　　　　　　　　スケ番

Certain girls want to stand out in Japan. Whether these girls ride with motorcycle gangs or hang out in the urban jungle, their outlandish clothes and rainbow-streaked hair demand attention. English speakers might call them delinquents, but Japanese slang terms them "boss girls" (*sukeban*), a nasty contraction of *suke*, the word gangsters use for their female companions, and "gang leader" (*bancho*). These boss girls lead the increasing number of Japanese girls who are caught engaging in antisocial or criminal behavior.

Japanese can pick out a potential *sukeban* on the basis of defiant acts so subtle that Westerners would term them self-expression. For example, pamphlets printed by Japanese police in the 1980s include sketches of girls in school uniforms demonstrating such "omens of downfall" as colored socks, rolled-up sleeves, permed hair, and lengthened skirts. In Japan's extremely homogeneous society, even these minor dress-code violations become significant. Schools, especially private ones, often have elaborate rules governing their students' appearance and behavior both in and out of school, and they send employees to coffee shops and movie theaters to check for violators. The *sukeban* use peer group pressure to enforce their equally strict nonconformist dress code of flamboyance.

From the craving to stand out, Japanese delinquent girls may progress to any combination of the following offenses: glue sniffing, stimulant drug use, prostitution, shoplifting, extortion, theft, and violence. The ratio of females among Japan's juvenile delinquents rose from under ten percent in 1965 to nineteen percent in 1981, with violent behavior showing an especially sharp increase. Delinquent girls also have proliferated in the fantasies of Japanese boys. Many boys' comic books now glorify the exploits of wayward boys and their sleazy, rowdy *sukeban* buddies. Comics aimed at girls tell no such tales.

If a girl is apprehended in Japan, she most likely will be charged with pre-delinquency (*guhan*). The character for "crime" (*han*) is prefaced by one for "anxiety" (*gu*), expressing the fears of authorities. Many girls at the nation's Classification Centers for Youth, the first stop in a youth's passage through the corrections system, have been classified under this uniquely Japanese legal concept. The law defines a pre-delinquent as someone prone to commit a crime because she or he habitually disobeys the reasonable rules of parents, runs away from home without reason, associates with known criminals, frequents places of dubious reputation, or habitually acts in ways that endanger morality. It seems that *guhan* could be a license for police to arrest any kid deemed suspicious, but authorities generally use it in the opposite way: as a milder charge to avoid stigmatizing youths who have committed more serious crimes, such as prostitution.

tekireiki   The Right Age   適 齢 期

"She's the right age" opens a spectrum of possibilities as wide and colorful as a peacock's tail in English, but in Japanese it almost always means one thing. She's reached marriageable age. *Tekireiki*, literally "suitable age," also applies to men old enough to marry in Japan. This concept is so important that there are several other ways to say it, including "about that age" (*toshigoro*) and the more direct "marriage period" (*konki*). The appropriate age varies by gender. Physically, women's reproductive prime is shorter than men's, but the concept of *tekireiki* is briefer than biology demands.

Nowadays, many people consider women's "right age" to last from twenty-three to twenty-five, while men are expected to wait until they have established some seniority and savings at age twenty-five to twenty-eight. The vast majority of Japanese marriages do, indeed, fall during these peak periods, though women are marrying later than in the past. Grooms' ages have remained stable, while the average bride has aged from 23.2 years old in 1930 to 25.3 in 1982. The concept of a "right age" is reinforced by health textbooks used in Japanese schools, though they do grant more leeway than popular wisdom allows. "*Tekireiki* for marriage in our country is generally said to be about twenty to thirty-four for men and twenty to twenty-nine for women," states one. Japanese law also draws the line differently for brides and grooms, recognizing only marriages of girls over sixteen and boys over eighteen.

A Japanese woman who doesn't marry when the time is ripe risks being ridiculed by such words as "Christmas cake" (*Kurisumasu keeki*). In the weeks leading up to Christmas and on Christmas day, Japanese munch a frothy strawberry shortcake decorated with Santas and such. Women are likened to these concoctions in Japanese slang because nobody wants either one after the twenty-fifth.

Although *tekireiki* usually applies to matrimony, Japanese tradition says there is a right age for just about everything. When a baby girl is exactly thirty days old, for example, she is the right age for presentation to the deities residing at the local shrine. (Baby boys should be thirty-one days old.) When she is three, she joins three-year-old boys in dressing up to make another auspicious shrine visit, which traditionally marks their passage from babyhood to childhood. This fashion festival for tykes is called Three-Five-Seven (*shichi-go-san*) because five-year-old boys and seven-year-old girls also participate, commemorating the ages at which they were allowed to wear their first formal clothing in the Edo period. For a girl, this meant replacing her loose sash with the stiff, wide belt called *obi*.

Where there are right ages, there are also wrong ones. When women hit one of the female "unlucky years" (*yaku-doshi*)—

nineteen and the even more dreaded thirty-three—they are supposed to avoid any major undertaking, from marriage to overseas
travel. (Men's unlucky ages are twenty-five, forty-two, and sixty.)
At these ages, some people take precautions by visiting a shrine
to receive a blessing or lucky amulet.

3

Hey, Mrs. Interior
MARRIED LIFE

TARO

"Returnees" (*demodori*) can't really return to the place they used to be. The women called *demodori* may still follow the tradition of moving back in with their parents, but they can never fully revert to their former respectable status because they are divorced. Reduced job opportunities and hostile public opinion face anyone, female or male, who has gotten a divorce. A 1984 government survey found that two-thirds of Japanese don't believe in divorce as a solution for an unhappy marriage.

General terms such as divorce (*rikon*) can apply to either gender, but the Japanese never call men returnees because, theoretically, they never left home in the first place. Although divorce in Japan today differs sharply from what it was in pre-industrial times, people still hark back to olden days when they use the mildly disapproving term *demodori*. Divorce used to entail deleting the wife's name from her husband's family register and sending her away, whereupon, as the word *demodori* implies, she would have nowhere to go but back to her own parents' place. "Women have no home in the three worlds" (*Onna wa sangai ni ie nashi*), says a proverb the Japanese borrowed from China. In Buddhist thought, the three worlds that comprise all of existence are the realms of desire, form, and formlessness. Most Japanese have a more down-to-earth interpretation: Women always live in homes owned by their fathers, husbands, and sons.

No matter what fault she found in her husband, a Japanese bride could not request divorce from the thirteenth to nineteenth centuries. Her only alternative was to run away to a "refuge temple" (*kakekomi-dera*), also called a "divorce temple" (*enkiri-dera*). Her refuge kept her safe from her husband, but she could neither remarry nor even see her own children until she had either passed three years there or received his consent to divorce. Many men agreed to divorce their runaway wives, although the nun's life was so strict that some women fled back with new appreciation for their husbands. After the long wait or the husband's approval, a woman could take a new mate. The children from her previous marriage generally remained in their father's custody. It was 1873 before Japanese women attained the right to request divorce. Under the civil code passed in 1898, women could divorce on the grounds of cruelty, desertion, or serious misconduct, but not adultery. On the other hand, the code said female infidelity could be punished with both a divorce and a two-year jail sentence. This was still an improvement over the Edo-period sentence for unfaithful wives: death.

All a husband needed to do to obtain a divorce during the Edo period was have a note delivered to his wife or her guardian saying that he wanted to separate. The divorce letters were so short that they came to be called "three-and-a-half lines" (*mikudarihan*). Women who saw the ominous notes understood instantly, even if they were illiterate. A widely read eighteenth-century book on morality, *Onna Daigaku* (Greater Learning for Women) reiterated the seven reasons for divorcing a wife that were first codified by the Japanese in the eighth century: disobedience, sterility, lewdness, jealousy, leprosy or other serious illness, stealing, and prattling disrespectfully.

When divorcing was so easy, it was also common. Japan's divorce rate was higher at the turn of the century than the rates that alarmed social analysts in the mid-1980s. Government statistics show the number of divorces per thousand people rose steadily from 1963 to 1983, then began to decline. The post–World War II peak of 1.5 is still far below the level of the late nineteenth century. From 1882 to 1897, there was an average of 2.8 divorces per thousand people.

Today's divorcee is a far cry from the *demodori* who shuddered every time she spotted a three-and-a-half-line note. Three out of four contemporary divorces are requested by the wife, who usually retains custody of the children. Ninety percent of divorces are granted after the wife and husband agree on terms and submit a request to the government. The rest are decided by a family court. She is likely to receive a one-time alimony payment, called "consolation money" (*isharyo*). Only one or two out of ten divorced mothers receive regular child support payments. Men can remarry immediately, while women are legally bound to wait six months to determine the paternity of future offspring.

The returnee mentality extends to surnames as well. While Western women fought for the right to reclaim their maiden names after divorce, Japanese faced the opposite problem. Until 1976, a wife (or husband) who had assumed the spouse's surname upon marriage was required by law to return to the premarital name after splitting up. The name switch signaled the disgraceful status to everyone, and a child whose parent had a different surname encountered discrimination. Now, by notifying their local mayor within three months of divorce, Japanese who don't like the returnee label can at least avoid the return to their original name.

gokiburi teishu   Cockroach Husbands   ゴキブリ亭主

What could be more useless, annoying, and downright repulsive than a cockroach in the kitchen? A husband in the kitchen, says the majority of conventional Japanese women who cooked up the slang term "cockroach husband" (*gokiburi teishu*) to repel the men who threaten to invade their territory. They reason that meal preparation actually takes longer with the "help" of any inexperienced cook. Traditionally, the kitchen is one place Japanese women feel no pressure to bolster the male ego. Many regard it as their sanctuary. Until recent times, men gladly relinquished the right to cook, if need be quoting the proverb "A gentleman will not enter the kitchen" (*Danshi chubo ni irazu*).

Most of today's housewives do not complain about men going out to work while women run the homes. A 1983 government survey found 71 percent of Japanese women favored this arrangement, many more than the 56 percent in the Philippines and 34 percent in the United States. The number of Japanese females who are unlatching the kitchen door is increasing, though; 83 percent favored the traditional division of labor in 1972. Government statistics confirm that the ideal is changing more rapidly than the real. The average Japanese woman spent three hours and twenty-three minutes per day on housekeeping and child care in 1981, while the typical man devoted eight minutes to it.

However, cockroach husbands are not limited to the kitchen. Any time her mate displeases her, a Japanese wife could whip out the insult. Men cannot fight back on the same terms, for there is no "cockroach wife." The word is so broad that nowadays some free thinkers might even call a fellow a cockroach for *not* helping with kitchen chores. Enough couples are challenging the status quo by sharing housework that Japanese have recently invented a half-joking word equivalent to the English "househusband." Pronounced *shufu*, it sounds the same as the common word for housewife, but instead of the usual "main lady," the characters spell "main husband."

This word for housewife, like many words for wives in general, used to be a term of rank. It was a luxury for women to be able to devote themselves to housework before modernization began in 1868. Then, for the first time in Japanese history, homes shifted from being centers of production to bases for consumption and bringing up children. Along with this change came several new words to aggrandize the limited pursuits of the new generation of housewives: *kaji* (housework), *ikuji* (child care), and *ryori* (cookery). A label also had to be coined for the large population of new housewives. They were dubbed *shufu*. Until the end of World War II, the term was only applied to the woman who represented the household within the family system, but now it means any housewife. When the popular women's magazine *Shufu no Tomo* (Housewife's Companion) was founded in the early twentieth century, its title was as innovative as America's *Ms.* magazine.

A few househusbands are beginning to enter the world of stove and sink. Recipe columns for men are published under such titles as "Kitchen Papa" in many Japanese men's magazines and newspapers, including even the staid *Nihon Keizai Shinbun*, probably Japan's closest equivalent to the *Wall Street Journal*. At least one of Tokyo's major bookstores has concocted a "Cookbooks for Men" section. Boys are not required to take home economics classes in school, but some women's groups are agitating for that change. Men who find cooking fun got together in Tokyo in 1977 to form the "Let's-Put-Gentlemen-in-the-Kitchen Club" (*danshi chubo ni hairo kai*), which boasted five hundred members in that city alone eight years after its founding. As part of its non-sexist philosophy, the club admits both genders. Female membership was twenty percent in the mid-1980s and growing. More than one liberated young woman has used the club to find a husband who was ready, willing, and able to share kitchen duty.

The trend should provide practical benefits to men as well as women, if there's any truth in a favorite legend whispered in the kitchen enclaves. Housewives love to repeat variations on the tale of the man who outlived his wife—only to starve because he didn't know how to cook, how to use a can opener, nor even where to find the food. Cockroaches, at least, know their way around the kitchen.

kafu ni somaru
To Become Dyed in the Family Ways 　　　　　家風に染まる

Japanese brides wear white in one part of the wedding ceremony—not only to symbolize their purity, but also, some say, to show they are as blank as an empty sheet of paper or a swath of colorless cloth. They are ready "to be dyed in the family ways" (*kafu ni somaru*) of their husband's home. The "dyeing" begins with simple adjustments such as cooking style. Meals must be made sweeter or saltier, more Westernized or based on regional recipes, whatever suits the family taste. Other modifications come harder. The new bride is supposed to socialize with friends—or not socialize—according to the patterns set by her in-laws. If women in the family don't work outside the home, she is discouraged from holding a job. On the other hand, if everyone pitches in with the family business, they expect her to join in, too. The task of enforcing the transformation usually falls to the mother-in-law.

Another term for this process is "to be dyed in the *ie*" (*ie ni somaru*). *Ie*, which is also the first character in *kafu*, means the family, the house, the household, the genealogy, and more, for it was the official foundation of Japanese social organization from feudal times until the end of World War II. Under the system, brides left their own *ie* to be thrust into the strong dye of their new homesteads. Usually each *ie* was headed by an oldest son and consisted of his wife and descendants. Younger sons were raised to be colorful enough to start their own offshoot *ie*.

Under the old *ie* system, a woman could be easily divorced if a tinge of independence showed through and marred her new coloring. The importance of family ways is reflected in turn-of-the-century letters of divorce which made such agonizingly vague accusations as "she doesn't match the family ways" (*kafu ni awanai*). Some people still admonish women that their duty is to "guard the *ie*" (*ie o mamoru*), which implies both staying in the house and upholding its ways.

The marital relationship in Japan solidifies into a reality that can be seen and touched: "husband-and-woman teacups" (*meoto-jawan*). The two cups are identical except in size, and the bigger cup belongs to the man. *Meoto-jawan* originated with the merchant class at the end of the Edo period, and then became high fashion early in this century. Some say that the first his-and-hers cups were of the same dimensions, but that the male mug was enlarged gradually, in keeping with the cultural climate. Similarly, social norms in other nations have forced Japanese to equalize some export models of *meoto-jawan*. And when it comes to buying their own Western teacups, which have handles while the Asian type do not, Japanese gladly buy what they call pair cups (*pea kappu*) of equal proportion.

Other traditional eating utensils also come in odd-sized pairs designed for married couples. These include the rice bowls that are also called *meoto-jawan* and the chopsticks known as *meoto-bashi*. In feudal days, many husbands actually did consume more and better food than their wives. Mealtime custom decreed that the woman of the house would first dish out the choicest morsels to the top-ranking man, then proceed down the pecking order. Children got to eat their fill, because the needs of their growing bodies were recognized. The people fed last and sometimes least were young brides.

Meoto-jawan sets continue to be a common gift for married couples, especially newlyweds. Such a gift not only suggests that the man gets more, but also that the married couple is a single, permanent unit with the same taste. Nobody ever splits the his-and-hers cups to sell or give in mixed pairs or individually, though a spouse might drink from one when the "other half" is away. Inseparability combines with size difference to inspire people to stick the label of *meoto*, which literally means "husband and female," onto various natural phenomena. Two boulders resting together are declared "husband and woman rocks" (*meoto iwa*). When Japanese see two pine trees entwined, they call them "husband and woman pines" (*meoto matsu*). Sometimes they pray to such trees for help in making a good marriage match.

One item that does not come in husband-and-wife pairs is the kimono. Now that Western clothing is the norm, young Japanese couples sometimes appear in look-alike sweat shirts, tennis outfits, and the like. Western notions of his-and-hers clothing, designed for dating couples as well as married ones, were readily embraced by a culture that has been using *meoto* objects for centuries.

Meshi! Furo! Neru!   Food! Bath! Bed!   飯・風呂・寝る

Three little words are exchanged nightly between husbands and wives in Japan. The typical Tokyo salaried worker arrives home between 9 and 10 P.M., exhausted from an hour on the commuter train and still slightly tipsy from the obligatory drinking bout after work. "*Meshi!*" he orders, using a crude word for food, and his wife scurries to bring his meal. When he is full, he says, "*Furo!*" She nods. She has already prepared his bath. After he emerges from the steamy tub, he speaks again: "*Neru!*" Time for his wife to roll out the futon bedding. Wives often joke ruefully that their husbands are so busy contributing to Japan's economic miracle that these are the only three words the men ever say to them. "*Meshi! Furo! Neru!*" has become a cliché for the lot of a salaried man and his wife.

On the other hand, Japanese wives and husbands don't really want to hear the three little words that Western couples find so important, "I love you." Most couples never utter the phrase at all. Japanese and Western observers have come up with a variety of explanations for this silence. They point out that Japanese tradition says marriage is primarily an economic arrangement for continuing the family line, and adding love to the equation is likely to do more harm than good. This concept may still influence people, and some loveless couples do stick together for the sake of the children, but most Japanese marrying today tell others they do it for love. However, saying "I love you" feels embarrassing and needless. Embarrassment is said to stem from the idea that a married couple is one body, not two individuals. This may also explain why Japanese parents do not profess love to their kids. When a husband and wife feel so intimately connected, expressing love is like praising oneself, a taboo in Japanese culture. Direct words are unnecessary and may limit and devalue the emotion they strive to express. In Japan, which is permeated by the less-is-more aesthetic of haiku poetry, love is conveyed by countless subtle gestures and expressions. Sometimes all that needs to be said is "*Meshi! Furo! Neru!*"

mukoyoshi   Adopted Sons-in-Law   婿 養 子

When Japanese wed, the law snatches the surname from one spouse and forces both to answer to the same family name. People who think names should be untouched by marriage have formed the Group to Promote Separate Family Names, which conducted a survey in 1985 that found forty percent of women who took their husbands' names were reluctant to do so. However, unlike many Western societies, Japan does not automatically expect the wife to relinquish her name. A minority of Japanese men have been assuming their wives' family names since time immemorial.

These rare birds are called "adopted sons-in-law" (*mukoyoshi* or just *yoshi*). They comprise less than two percent of Japanese husbands, but they receive social approval mixed with pity as conformists within an ancient institution. If a family has no sons, tradition says the husband of the eldest daughter should take her surname and be adopted as an heir. Occasionally families choose to adopt a groom in other circumstances, such as when natural sons are too young or profligate to head the household, or when a daughter is too beloved to be "given away." Family business owners are especially eager for the new son-in-law to accept their name as well as their wealth because customers and employees tend to have more confidence in a boss whose surname is identical to his firm's trade name. Naturally, the people most concerned about heirs are the ones with something worth inheriting: a family business, a fortune, or at least a name with an aristocratic history. Thus, *mukoyoshi* are sometimes snubbed as crass opportunists who marry for money, a feat that is praised when women do it as "riding the jeweled palanquin" (*tamanokoshi ni noru*). Unlike the gold digger or fortune hunter despised by English speakers who think love is the point of marriage, the Japanese female who makes it into that luxurious palanquin gets public acclaim for achieving one of the highest goals traditionally expected of women.

After the wedding, the adopted son-in-law is supposed to

become a member of his new clan. Instead of getting his own way like most Japanese men, he tends to conform to their "family ways" just like a typical Japanese bride. Some even shock their male buddies by using polite language to address the wives to whom they owe their names.

Today computerized matchmakers' memory banks store the vital statistics of many *mukoyoshi*-seekers, often the daughters of farmers or independent businessmen. For example, the Altmann System, Japan's oldest and largest computer go-between, maintains a data base in which about ten percent of the women are hunting *mukoyoshi*. Fortunately, only sixty-five percent of the men on file find this prospect "impossible." The proportion of computerized *mukoyoshi* stalkers is higher than in the overall population, for such women must resort to extraordinary means to find a man to take their name. Tradition sanctions the *mukoyoshi*, but he still loses face when he drops his name.

naijo no ko   Success from Inside Help   内助の功

One important factor in Japan's economic achievement is ignored by most Western analysts. It is "success from inside help" (*naijo no ko*). When various Japanese terms for corporate management techniques are explicated in detail, this hidden resource that makes it all possible is often omitted. As usual in Japan, the helpful "insider" is none other than the wife. *Naijo no ko* means a man's success resulting from the aid and sacrifices of his spouse.

Without wives who handle the family meals, clothes, and finances, Japanese married men would be unable to continue working as long and hard as they do to maintain economic growth. (Company dormitories provide many of these services to single men and, sometimes, women.) Language further affirms that Japanese wives play an essential role in their mates' accomplishments with the word "wife role" (*nyobo yaku*). A man who is always ready to support and advise a friend or coworker, the reliable sort called a "right-hand man" by English speakers, is complimented as a "wife role" in Japan.

At a national level, Japanese women come to the rescue in a similar way. Almost all the people representing the nation's business and government outside Japan are male, while back home on the "inside" women shoulder the unglamorous but essential jobs such as office work and computer chip inspection. This is not a new policy. Women comprised an average sixty percent of the factory labor force from 1894 to 1912, a crucial period in Japan's early industrialization.

Ask any Japanese about *naijo no ko*, and she or he is likely to reply with the story of a famous feudal family in Shikoku called Yamanouchi. History books praise Mrs. Yamanouchi, saying that the rise in the family's fortunes can be traced back to Kazutoyo Yamanouchi (1546–1605) and his clever wife Kenshoin (1557–1617). The tale began when the local warlord was planning an inspection of his troops. Kazutoyo discovered that a peerless steed was for sale—at a stupendous price. He was lamenting the poverty that prevented him from buying the horse sure to impress his lord when his wife pulled out that exact sum of money from the handle of her mirror and handed it to him. Kazutoyo was stunned. The family had been scrimping by on the barest necessities of food and clothing. His thrifty wife explained that her father gave her the funds when they married for use in an emergency, such as the need for a horse. From her seed money, he went on to win the respect of his superiors, triumph in many battles, and eventually gain wealth and power for their entire clan.

nomi no fufu   Flea Couples   蚤の夫婦

"Flea couple" (*nomi no fufu*) does not mean a pair of tiny insects, but a wife standing taller than her husband. Women are expected to be shorter than their mates in Japan, where rigid standards of propriety exist for almost every situation. Any size reversal makes people nervously remember that males are usually bigger in the animal kingdom, except in the case of fleas.

Women feel even more itchy about the height ratio than men. Japan's largest computerized matchmaker figured in the mid-1980s that husband-hunters' ideals averaged out to a man who is about eight inches taller. Meanwhile, the men were dreaming of that special someone only four inches shorter. The gap is explained by the fact that women take their high-heeled shoes into consideration.

Females are also on the lookout for men who tower over them

in terms of years. A 1983 government survey of Japanese singles aged eighteen to thirty-four found that most respondents thought a husband should be three years older than his wife. About thirty percent of men and twenty percent of women said the ideal age difference was five or more years. Only a few put forward the opposite ideal of a woman marrying a younger man, supporting the proverb which advises, "Have a wife one year older, even if you must wear iron sandals to find her" (*Hitotsu masari no nyobo wa kane no waraji de sagashite mo mote*). The idea is that an older woman will mother her husband, taking such good care of him and his household that he should use steely determination in searching for her. However, when these uncommon matches are made, any female older than her husband is branded in colloquial speech with the totally unromantic term "big-sister wife" (*anesan nyobo*).

okusan   Mrs. Interior   奥さん

Whether they are at home, at work, or outdoors, married women in Japan are addressed as "Mrs. Interior" (*okusan* or, more formally, *okusama*). *Okusan* is the most common word for talking to or about other men's spouses—one of many situations with its own specialized wife vocabulary in Japanese. *Oku* means not just interior, but the depths far within a building. The suffixes *-san* and *-sama* are not gender specific, but broad enough to mean Mr., Mrs., or even Ms. However, *okusan* can never be used to denote a Mr. Interior, no matter how much time he spends in the deepest recesses of his home. As the language makes clear, that is traditionally considered the woman's place.

The term is rooted in pre-industrial Japan, where the wives of lords were exalted as *okusama*. While most feudal women labored with their families to wring a living from farmland, the aristocratic *okusama* enjoyed homes big enough to have an *oku*, and leisure enough to spend time there. The original *okusama* were not only cloistered in the house, but kept hostage in the feudal capital of Edo (present-day Tokyo) as part of an elaborate system of social control that lasted over two hundred years in the Edo period. Called "alternate attendance" (*sankin kotai*), it required lords to troop back and forth every other year between their hometowns and the houses in Edo where their wives lived. Industrialization broke down that system and gave rise to salaried men able to support their wives. Such women were likened to the spouses of feudal lords, and *okusama* was on its way to losing its snob appeal. Like the English word "lady," *okusama* has been vulgarized into an all-purpose term for women. For conversing with or about other people's husbands, the current male equivalent of *okusan* is "honorable master" (*goshujin* or *danna-san*). These terms for husbands are used even now in discussions of slavery as well.

When they talk about their own spouses, Japanese use a set of terms that is different, though some core meanings are similar. A man ordinarily refers to his own wife as "house-insider" (*kanai*) or, more informally, as *nyobo*, the word for court ladies' quarters. She, in turn, describes him without honorifics as "master" (*shujin* or *danna*), or more informally as *teishu*, which can also refer to the master of an inn or teahouse. Yet another pair of terms usually comes into play outside conversation, in written and legalistic or formal Japanese. Wives, one's own or otherwise, are termed *tsuma*, written with a character depicting a woman holding a broom. Similarly, all husbands are designated *otto*, a character that shows somebody wearing the ornamental hairpin that used to signal coming-of-age for Japanese males.

Being super-polite can mean denigrating one's own spouse, along with everything else associated with oneself. To meet that need, the language is marbled like over-tender beef with fatuous terms such as "my foolish wife" (*gusai*) and what could be loosely translated as "little one" (*saikun*). Once in a while *gusai* is used to insult, but now mainly older men use it humbly in formal situations where they are forced to talk about their wives, especially when they make speeches at weddings. The closest that husbands come to such a demeaning designation is being called "innkeepers" (*yadoroku*), a term that implies they are loafers.

The concept of marriage as a Mrs. Interior wedded to her master rankles some Japanese. Recently some feminists have revived an old-fashioned term as a sexism-free alternative that applies equally to all spouses, male and female, one's own or another's. They suggest "life partner" (*tsureai*), based on an old verb for marrying that literally means to accompany (*tsureau*). The same characters are used to describe "allied" nations.

Choosing the right spousal term from this huge stockpile comes as naturally to Japanese as the distinction English speakers draw between calling a man "husband" to others and addressing him directly by name or as "dear." Japanese make that division, too. Today some egalitarian couples call each other by a form of their personal names, but traditionally that mode of address was considered disrespectful, appropriate when men spoke to their wives, but not in the reverse. Although men can call their wives by name without fear of offending, some opt for *oi!*, the equivalent of "hey!" To others, she is *omae* or *kimi*, words for "you" that in this context are near in nuance to "darling." Women also affectionately call their husbands "you" (*anata*), a word that scholars say originally may have meant either "that person" or "over there." However, the most common forms of address between spouses are "Mother" (*okaasan* or *mama*) and "Father" (*otosan* or *papa*), suggesting that the spouse relationship is often overshadowed by the parenting role. Within the traditional three-generation household, everyone tends to agree on one form of address for each family member. Once grandchildren are born, the grandmother bequeaths the term "Mom" to the children's mother.

oshidori fufu   Mandarin-Duck Couples   おしどり夫婦

The colorful mandarin ducks (*oshidori*) native to Japan always paddle in pairs, quacking encouragement to their mates. When a wife and husband seem to swim side-by-side, supporting each other's efforts, the Japanese call them a "mandarin-duck couple" (*oshidori fufu*). The buoyant image dates back to popular Japanese legends told more than seven centuries ago and influenced by poetry from another mandarin-duck habitat, China. In the thirteenth-century Japanese anthology *Kokon Chomonju*, a hunter kills an *oshidori* drake, then discovers its mate has died of grief. Touched, he lays down his weapons and takes holy orders. Today biologists dispassionately point out that mandarin-duck fidelity lasts for only a year, then the birds switch spouses. But the cold water of scientific logic just rolls off the backs of ordinary Japanese.

These happy pairs do not belong to the same flock that English speakers call "lovebirds." That implies lovers so deeply infatuated with each other that they cannot be happy unless they are together, like the lovebird parrots that people keep caged as pets. Mandarin-duck couples sail free and alert through society at large, just as their namesakes roam the wilds of Japan's marshes, streams, and ponds. A comparison of the couples called "mandarin ducks" and "lovebirds" also points out cross-cultural differences in the conduct of courtship and marriage. Western couples tend to act like lovebirds from the dating phase until after the honeymoon. On the other hand, *oshidori fufu* applies only to people already joined in matrimony because *fufu*, literally "husband and lady," cannot include unmarried pairs as the English word "couple" does. The words *oshidori fufu* conjure up a middle-aged wife and husband to many people in Japan, reflecting the traditional idea that marriage is arranged by parents to link two strangers who learn over the years how to live in harmony. This kind of twosome is also praised as "one heart, same body" (*isshin dotai*), a phrase that alarms some spouses who prefer the mandarin-duck image because they want to maintain their own identity and flight patterns.

The unsinkable metaphor is evolving with the times. Today Japan's gossip media tout younger versions of *oshidori fufu*. Marriages among Japanese stars who sing and act are proclaimed to be mandarin-duck couples when the wife continues her pop career. Magazines carry photographs of these dynamic duos attending parties together, still something of a rarity in Japanese social life.

oshikake nyobo   Intruder Wives   押し掛け女房

Most Japanese women wait for someone to ask their hand in marriage, but females seize the initiative often enough that a special term has developed to describe them. These assertive brides are "intruder wives" (*oshikake nyobo*), based on a word usually used for uninvited guests (*oshikake kyaku*). Often they are energetic women who set their hearts on indecisive men, then maintain the will and pep to lavish loving care on them after marriage. At least among women, the word arouses more admiration than blame, for an intruder wife must be brave to carry out her tactics.

Typically, she barges into her beau's home without permission and starts living there. She pampers him by cooking nightly feasts, cleaning up afterward without complaint, and keeping his apartment and clothes in top-notch order. He comes to depend on her more and more until he realizes he can't live without her. Before long, they are married. Although the more modest maidens of old did not intrude to the point of cohabitation, the technique of catching husbands by cooking, cleaning, and coddling has a long tradition in Japan.

Just because the indulgent intruder wives force their fellows to marry them doesn't necessarily mean they usurp the role of verbally asking for his hand. However, some Japanese women do issue marriage proposals. A government study determined that the women who are now old enough to be grandmothers were especially prone to pop the question. The survey of Japan's rural and suburban women showed that slightly more than ten percent proposed to men in the late 1940s, but the ratio of female proposers dropped steadily to hit three percent by the 1960s.

There is no such thing as an "intruder husband" in Japanese because it is taken for granted that the man will be the aggressor in the spouse hunt. Although men generally take the lead in suggesting marriage, they seldom use intrusive words to pop the question. The traditional phrase is "Will you follow me?" (*Boku ni tsuite kite kuremasu ka*). A poll by *Shukan Post* magazine in the mid-1980s showed most guys hint at the subject with ambiguous expressions like "Let's eat breakfast together every morning" or "When do you think you'll be quitting your job?"

otto o shiri ni shiku   To Sit on a Husband   夫を尻に敷く

If a woman refused her husband's request to make a sukiyaki dinner because she preferred eating tempura, Japanese would probably say she "sat on" him. The Japanese version of the henpecked husband is a man flattened out under his wife's massive buttocks. Wives who dominate are said to "sit on" (*shiri ni shiku*) their husbands, just as they would plop down on a cushion or a futon mattress, the context in which the sitting verb *shiku* is frequently heard. People usually convert the phrase to the passive voice, implying sympathy with the squashed spouse by saying "the husband is being sat upon" (*otto ga shiri ni shikareru*). The reference to the husband (*otto*) can be dropped because this negative expression always condemns bossy wives. *Shiri ni shiku* cannot refer to a boss who holds an underling under her or his thumb, or a mother who keeps her son tied to her apron strings.

Literally, *shiri ni shiku* means to flatten with the buttocks and hips, which are all encompassed in the word *shiri*. When the put-upon object is a cushion or bedding, the somewhat crude anatomical reference is generally omitted. The figure of speech includes the criticism that the woman's rump is too fat, otherwise her man would be able to topple her authority. However, skinny hips are no better. To say someone's "hips are light" (*shiri ga karui*) can be an accusation of instability, carelessness, or—only in the case of women—loose morals. These are just a few of the dozens of hip expressions used in Japan.

The spreading of husbands under the hips is also called "wife rule" (*kakaa-denka*). *Kakaa*, a nasty name for wives, is one of the few characters created by the Japanese instead of copied from the Chinese. It combines the ideograms for "female" and "nose" to concoct a foul-smelling term. The opposite extreme is *teishu kanpaku*, in which an informal word for husband is followed by a term for the emperor's chief advisor. Some Japanese women use *teishu kanpaku* with the same outrage that English speakers vent toward "male chauvinist pigs." However, since Japanese husbands traditionally have been expected to act like the king of the castle, husband rule can carry a good connotation, while being sat on by a wife inevitably sounds negative.

Among those who feel wife rule is getting out of hand are officials of the Japanese government. A 1985 guide to parents of three-year-olds authorized by the Ministry of Health and Welfare used the "sat upon" metaphor to urge fathers to be more active in child rearing and to show their kids what it means to be masculine. A cartoon in the guide pictures a bewildered son watching his father struggle to escape from beneath his mom's enormous posterior. The boy remembers the lyrics of an old military song lauding the brave, fallen soldiers of Japan: "Father, you were so strong!"

Inflation even affects slang for subservient husbands. The guys Japanese used to call "hundred-yen husbands" (*hyakuen teishu*) have been marked up to "thousand-yen husbands" (*senen teishu*) over the past few decades. Their personality remains the same. Such men hand their paychecks directly to their wives, then wait to be doled out a minimal daily allowance: a hundred yen in the 1960s, a thousand yen today. Either way, it is just enough to cover lunch and cigarettes. The word is insulting, not because the husband lets his wife control the money, but because he accepts a stingy amount.

There is no term "thousand-yen wife" in Japan. Handling the household budget was considered women's work in old Japan, and it still is in 83 percent of Japanese households, according to a 1984 government survey. The same study found that the larger the purchase, the less control wives have over it. For major electric appliances, 48 percent of couples made joint decisions, while 30 percent of husbands and 17 percent of wives made up their mind alone. The level of joint decision-making is almost identical when buying land and housing, but men are much more likely to determine to buy property on their own (38 percent) than their wives are (2 percent). Women point out that just because they decide when to buy a new refrigerator, and maybe even a new house, it doesn't mean they can make decisions on how to live their own life. For example, they may hesitate to spend the money on a tennis class for their own enjoyment, or in any other way that would displease the fellow who hands over his paycheck. Still, Japanese women seem to retain a psychological independence that allows them to call their husbands names that Western women never dreamed of, even during periods when their economic dependence was greatest. They aren't afraid to bluntly refer to their husbands as "wage delivery men" (*kyuryo unpannin*).

There are a few cases where the wife brings home the bacon to an unemployed mate. In the days when hairdressing was one of the best jobs open to women, any man who let a woman support him financially came to be disparaged as a "hairdresser's husband" (*kamiyui no teishu*), a term that lives on today.

Because Japanese women hold the purse strings, they are courted by corporations selling consumer products and investment opportunities. The people who crowd the loan and long-term deposit counters at Japanese banks are almost all fierce-looking women with gray hair and gray kimonos. Japanese advertisers have recognized that women exercise personal preferences even when shopping for the whole family, so they increasingly aim at women when promoting cars and computers, as well as food and fashions. Thanks to a new strategy by securities firms, some of the smiling door-to-door saleswomen in Japan now sell stocks and bonds instead of cosmetics.

yome ni iku   To Go as a Daughter-in-Law   嫁に行く

"Here comes the bride," the West's traditional wedding refrain, has a different ring in Japan. The bride (*hanayome* at the wedding, thereafter just *yome*) used to be expected to go irrevocably into her husband's home, never to return except for formal visits. Even today many women use the phrases "to go as a bride" (*yome ni iku*) or "to be kindly received" (*moratte morau*) to mean that they got married. The groom expresses his marriage by saying he "receives the bride" (*yome o morau* or *moratte yaru*). From the viewpoint of the bride's family, marriage means "to dispose of" (*katazukeru*) a daughter, a term never used for sons. Meanwhile, his family doesn't lose a son, but "takes a bride" (*yome o toru*) and thereby gains a daughter-in-law.

Yome is translated as "daughter-in-law" more often than "bride" because the newlywed woman often cannot concentrate on her relationship with the groom, but finds herself wedded to all his relatives. Even now, the *yome* is usually responsible for nursing her in-laws if they become bedridden or senile. The *yome* character itself expresses the whole concept admirably by melding the ideograms for "woman" and *ie*, which means both "house" and "family." This character is frequently converted into a verb, pronounced *totsugu*, that denotes a woman's "marrying into" her husband's house. The object of this verb is never a husband, but rather his family.

Matrimony was an alliance of two families until legal reforms of 1947 ordained that each couple start a new family register upon marriage. Prior to that, an important phase in the process was erasing the bride's name from her family register and entering it on the register of the groom's family. Especially if her mate was an eldest son, the *yome* entered the family home in the physical sense, too, and was expected to stay there, strictly following the ways and whims of her mother-in-law.

Marriage naturally came to be called *yome-iri*, "bride (or daughter-in-law) entrance," but during ancient matriarchal times, it was *muko-tori*, "taking a groom (or son-in-law)." Historical research shows that the word *yome* is new in comparison to *muko*. The concept of taking a son-in-law lives on today in about one out of fifty weddings, where the groom "enters" the bride's family as an adopted son-in-law (*mukoyoshi*) and assumes their name. The character for "family name" (pronounced *sei* or *sho*) reflects this by combining the ideograms for "female" and "life."

"Inserting a foot" (*ashi-ire*) is the name of another historical marriage pattern, whereby fiances slept together at one of their family homes for a period of time before officially marrying. In the case of female callers, they sometimes waited for pregnancy before holding the wedding. Scholars speculate that this trial marriage was a transitional form between matriarchal and patriarchal marriage systems. Once widespread among Japanese commoners, the practice of "inserting a foot" persisted into this century. Today a few free-thinking young couples live together (*dosei suru*), without the rest of the clan, before deciding to wed.

Now that every couple opens a new family register when they wed, all the words implying that women marry into their husband's family sound slightly old-fashioned. Newer terms include "tie-marriage" (*kekkon*) or the slang corrupted from the English sports term "to score a goal" (*goru-in suru*). Its use almost exclusively for wedding contrasts with the way English-speaking men use "score" to brag about sexual conquests.

Further assumptions underlying Japanese marriage are suggested by other synonyms applied only to one sex. Brides look at marriage as "eternal employment" (*eikyu shushoku*). Readily recognizing the economic basis of matrimony, they draw a parallel between choosing a mate and choosing a job. Only, unlike her husband, a Japanese wife can never retire from her work of caring for home and family. Men are the usual subject of a different wedding verb, "to stabilize oneself" (*mi o katameru*).

4

Honor That Bag
MOTHERHOOD

The "Fathers and Big Brothers Club" in Japan consists mostly of women. This patriarchal name clings to an activity that has long been the concern of mothers. To promote their children's education, parents join a school liaison group informally called *fukeikai*, literally "fathers and big brothers clubs." Many of the local groups have switched to calling themselves "fathers and mothers clubs" (*fubokai*) or "guardians clubs" (*hogoshakai*) because *fukei* is so obviously outmoded, but it is still in general use as a synonym for parent or guardian. Even more common is the sex-neutral term *oya*, which means parent without the legal responsibility of guardianship. Animals also have *oya*, but only people have *fukei*.

For much of Japan's more recent history, it was accurate to use "fathers and older brothers" as a synonym for legal guardians. Originally, Japanese women stayed in the homes of their foremothers to raise their children while a succession of husbands came and went. The ancient mother's control over her children was made manifest in incest laws. Marriage between children of the same father was acceptable, but if offspring of the same mother wed, they committed incest. The matriarchal social structure began declining in the seventh century, and women had no legal authority over their children's upbringing until reforms in the twentieth century. Female guardianship did not include the power to pass on nationality until 1984. Until then, the offspring of a Japanese man with a foreign wife were recognized as Japanese, but the children of a Japanese woman who wed a foreigner were denied citizenship.

Mothers aren't the only ones whose gender is disguised by old-boys-club terms like *fukei*. Every female identifies herself as one of the "brothers" when talking about her family. The word for sibling is *kyodai*, literally "older brothers and younger brothers." When asked how many *kyodai* they have—and the question comes up often in family-conscious Japan—guys automatically lump their sisters into the total, while a woman counts herself and her sisters among the brotherhood.

Japanese agree that "one princess, two fat fellow(s)" (*ichi hime, ni Taro*) embodies a time-honored ideal for the birth of their children. But try asking exactly what the ancients were advising in this proverb, and pandemonium breaks out.

Proponents of the most popular theory claim the saying refers to birth order. They say that the ideal first child is a girl, poetically referred to as "princess" (*hime*). Next, a boy is best. *Taro*, literally "fat fellow," indicates a son because it used to be one of the most common names given to boys, especially oldest sons. The advantage of having the "princess" first is based on the biological fact that girl babies are stronger and less likely to fall ill. These hardy girls are said to provide an extra bonus when Little Taro comes along, because they can help with the housework and child care, chores few Japanese think of ordering their sons to do.

Now that the average Japanese woman bears two children, compared to five before World War II, it is still popular to interpret the proverb as a recommended birth sequence. Another explanation is that it advocates a family of one daughter and two sons. The anonymous proverb-composers of old would have wanted more boys for a variety of reasons, including the fact that most sons proved useful on the farm, at war, and in the parents' old age, while the investment in rearing a daughter was usually lost when she married into another family. Modern Japanese still express a preference for sons.

When nature did not comply with the proverb, Japanese parents have been known to take matters into their own hands. Some poor, rural families were forced to resort to infanticide in order to survive, as recently as the late nineteenth century. This practice was called "thinning out" (*mabiki*), the same term used for weeding out some rice seedlings so the rest would have enough room and nourishment to thrive. Older offspring might be left to fend for themselves as "abandoned kids" (*sutego*). The victims were almost always female.

Most Japanese see no connection between infanticide and the little-girl faces on the wooden *kokeshi* dolls often sold as souvenirs. However, at least some Japanese propound a folk etymology that says *kokeshi* comes from "child (*ko*) erasure (*keshi*)," not "little poppies," the characters in accepted use today. According to this theory, the first *kokeshi* dolls were carved by parents to commemorate the daughters they had "erased."

mamagon   The Dreaded Mama-saurus   ママゴン

Mothers in Japan are often blamed for social problems ranging from school violence to public apathy. If only they would stop concentrating so much on their kids. Or, if only they would stop working outside the home and *start* concentrating on their kids....

While the social critics were exchanging high-flown words, modern kids invented one simple term for all bad mothers. They called them *mamagon*, meaning a mama who is as scary as a dinosaur. English speakers can borrow the dinosaur suffix to create "mama-saurus." Likewise, Japanese can invent words based on their monster suffixes: *-ra*, as in that famous cross between a whale (*kujira*) and a gorilla (*gorira*), Godzilla (*Gojira*); and *-gon*, as in the lesser known gobbler of money (*kane*), *Kanegon*. The ending is said to derive from the English word dragon. Adults don't use *mamagon*, but they know it, and they have been known to tease back with words such as "baby-saurus" (*bebiigon* or *bebiira*). *Papagon* is also possible, though less common. Like most of the slang young people sling around, the *gon* words have gone out of style now that adults have caught on to them.

Probably the most notorious species of *mamagon* is the "education mama" (*kyoiku mama*) often portrayed in the mass media. Barred by their gender from most public achievements, these women strive for vicarious success by driving their children to get good grades. They have made cram schools for kindergarten entrance exams into big business in Japan, though the system could not exist without the support of educational authorities and elite corporations that hire only from top universities. The husbands of education mamas are accomplices through their very lack of interest in their offspring's education. Women's almost total domination of this realm was measured by a 1984 government survey that showed half of Japanese mothers making all decisions about their kids' discipline or education, while only four percent of dads made a move without consulting the mother. Most Japanese fathers load all the responsibility for the children's education onto their wives, then blame the women if a child's test scores are poor.

Couples who relate to each other in this way appear to have little in common, and a proverb illuminates what keeps such marriages intact: "The child is the clasp" (*Ko wa kasugai*). A *kasugai* is not only the clasp at the bottom of a folding fan, but also the bolt locking the window shutters together. Obviously, the role of holding the parents' marriage together can place tremendous pressure on the children. An increasing number are releasing it in violence at school or in the home, where mothers are the most common victims.

Japanese mothers could congratulate themselves for the nation's high literacy rate and accompanying benefits, but an international survey showed that they aren't resting on their laurels. Far from it. The Japan Youth and Juvenile Research Institute questioned thousands of mothers in Japan and the United States in 1985 to discover that only eight percent of American moms doubted they were good mothers. Perhaps discouraged by social criticism aimed their way, fifty-seven percent of Japanese mothers suspected they might be *mamagon*.

mizugo   Unseeing Water-Babies   水 子

Thousands of Japanese women visit temples every year to bring baby clothes, cookies, toys, and other offerings to their *mizugo*, a word that has homonyms meaning either "water-baby" or "unseeing baby." In both cases, the *mizugo* is a fetus, removed from the watery warmth of the womb by nature or abortionist before it sees the world. "To make a water-baby" (*mizugo ni suru*) means to have an abortion. Several hundred years ago, the word *mizugo* also included small children who died within a few months of birth.

During the Edo period, people buried their water-babies under their homes, prayed for their souls to be reborn into the family again, and erected statues of child-guarding Buddhas near fields and mountains. Buddhist temples such as Tokyo's Shojuin have accepted offerings on behalf of the *mizugo* for centuries. Shojuin will provide a wooden tablet and incense for only a couple dollars, but in recent years more than two thousand temples and pseudo-temples have begun cashing in on the guilt feelings of people who rejected parenthood, especially women. The hallmark of these temples is the mini-forest of hot-pink pinwheels stuck in the ground to amuse and comfort the spirits of the fetuses whose ashes may be kept there. Unscrupulous temples charge as much as 150,000 yen ($1,000) to add one more figure to the crowd of *mizugo*-guarding Buddhas that are small enough to sit on the palm of a hand.

Women in Japan, as in other nations, sometimes feel that carrying out a legal abortion of their own choice is a necessary evil. Their sadness can be compounded by the fact that Japanese do not always draw a clear distinction between a fetus and a baby. Instead of saying "abort a fetus" (*taiji o orosu*), the more common object of the abortion verb is baby (*akachan*) or child (*kodomo*). These guilt feelings can be expelled—or exacerbated—by religious rites for the *mizugo*. Japanese Buddhism generally opposes abortion, and Shinto teaches that the soul of an aborted fetus can gain retribution by cursing its mother. Some temples post prominent signs listing the bad luck that befalls those who fail to placate the souls of their *mizugo* by paying the temple to perform memorial services. The ugliest threat is that subsequent children will be born with handicaps. Public disapproval of abortion is reflected in the *Mainichi* newspaper's National Opinion Survey on Family Planning for 1986, which showed only 16 percent of the women surveyed approved it unconditionally, while 66 percent approved under certain conditions and 13 percent disapproved.

Despite the fact that Japanese hesitate to approve of abortion, they are apt to undergo the operation. In fact, Japan's legal abortion rate is among the highest in the world. Japan's 1980 rate of 84.2 abortions per 1,000 women aged fifteen to forty-four gave it the third highest rate out of twenty-eight nations, behind only the Soviet Union and Rumania, according to the Population Council, a research and service organization based in New York City. This is about four times more than the official government figure; one explanation is that many doctors underreport these operations to escape taxation. Researchers estimate the average Japanese woman aborts two *mizugo* in her lifetime, usually after she is married.

Among the forces causing so many Japanese to continue using

a method they don't fully endorse is the fact that abortion is readily available, while the highly effective birth control pill is not. Most people rely on condoms and the rhythm method for birth control, then resort to abortion to remedy the relatively frequent contraceptive failures. This system is not opposed by most doctors, who make more profit by performing abortions than they would by prescribing pills, fitting diaphragms, or providing other modern alternatives.

Abortionists are certified by the government and they become members of what is called, without irony, the Motherhood Protection Association. The group's name, along with the references to the "mother's body" (*botai*) in Japan's abortion law, suggest the common Japanese attitude that the best reason for having an abortion is to protect the health of the woman, especially if she is the mother of at least one child, and her family is low on money. The physical or "economic reasons" clause in Japanese abortion law accounts for more than ninety-nine percent of abortions today. The current law can be traced back to the National Eugenic Law of 1940, patterned after eugenics-based laws in Nazi Germany. It allowed abortion only to eliminate genetic defects or save the mother's life. After World War II, the number of pregnancies in Japan swelled, as did the number of infanticides and black-market abortions, then called "descent from the womb" (*datai*). Under these circumstances, a new statute entitled Eugenic Protection Law (*yusei hogo ho*) was enacted in 1948 to vastly increase the rationales for legal abortion, which is formally termed "interruption" (*chuzetsu*). That law, with some revisions, remains in effect.

Bearing an unwanted child and giving it up for adoption is not a popular alternative. Each year ninety thousand Japanese become adopted children (*yoshi*). However, two-thirds of them are adults, often men adopted by their in-laws when they marry into the family. Most of the remainder are kids adopted by the new parent when a widow or divorcee remarries. Only a few are given up for adoption at birth. The phenomenon is a result of the easy access to abortion, compounded by the fact that a "not-yet-married mother" (*mikon no haha*) must list illegitimate births on her family register, an important document sometimes demanded by potential employers and even would-be spouses. The percentage of illegitimate babies among all births is lower in Japan than almost anywhere in the world. Until a legal reform in 1987, the biological mother's name also remained on her baby's family register after adoption.

obi iwai   Bellyband Celebrations   帯 祝 い

The modern, Western-style maternity clothes popular with pregnant Japanese women today may hide not only bulging bellies, but also time-honored ideas and customs. Many Japanese mothers-to-be, especially in rural areas, still wrap their abdomens in the traditional bellyband (*obi*) decorated by hand with festive characters. Doctors agree with folk wisdom that says the bellyband supports, warms, and protects the growing fetus. At least since the Muromachi period, older female relatives or friends have presented pregnant women with the long, cotton maternity under-sash at parties called "bellyband celebrations" (*obi iwai*). This red-and-white or pure white bellyband is termed an *iwata obi* to distinguish it from the shorter, more colorful *obi* worn outside a kimono. Today *iwata* is written with the characters "rock field" in the hope that the child will be as strong as a rock, but the term originally came from "purified-skin *obi*" because the *obi* was purified in religious rites. In the past, female relatives or a midwife showed the pregnant woman how to wrap it like an extended bandage binding her belly. Then they were likely to share a feast featuring red rice with kin and neighbors.

Today's bellyband celebrations usually occur in a hospital. The tradition of the expectant woman's mother providing the bellyband is dying out now that more women go with their husbands to obtain the *obi* from a shrine, temple, or store. They then bring it to a hospital, where a doctor brushes on characters such as "celebration," "safe delivery," or possibly "dog." The canine connection is that dogs supposedly have easy deliveries. The ceremony is generally scheduled on the Day of the Dog by the Chinese calendar in the fifth month of pregnancy by Japanese reckoning, which is what Westerners consider the fourth month. The bellyband celebration serves as confirmation both that the woman is expecting a baby and that her pregnancy is likely to progress smoothly, since most miscarriages occur in the first three months after conception.

Girded by their bellybands, Japanese women can choose from a variety of other folklore precautions to ensure the birth of a healthy, happy baby. The more common taboos are expressed in proverbs. "If a pregnant woman looks at a fire, her child will have a birthmark" (*Ninpu ga kaji o miru to umareru ko ni aza ga dekiru*). "If a pregnant woman eats rabbit, her child will have a harelip" (*Ninpu ga usagi o taberu to mitsukuchi no ko ga umareru*). A fetus will never form bones in the womb of a woman who nibbles octopus and other boneless seafood, while mothers-to-be who scrub their bathrooms daily will bear pretty babies. The list goes on and on. Many young women today have never even heard of these superstitions, but the belief that a woman's behavior during pregnancy can enhance her child's mental development lives on in the commonly known word "uterus education" (*tai-kyo*). It is defined as the education a child absorbs while in its mother's womb. The idea is that a woman can start teaching her child before it is born by listening to beautiful music, looking at fine artwork, reading great literature, or even studying English conversation.

The standard term for an expectant mother is *ninpu*, literally "pregnant lady." The same character for pregnant, which combines the ideograms for woman and conception, is the basis of the noun "pregnancy" (*ninshin*) and the verbs "to become pregnant" (*ninshin suru*) and "to impregnate" (*ninshin saseru*). Other common verbs suggest that life begins at conception; Japanese borrow the verb for hotel service to say "a life is lodging" (*inochi ga yadoru*). Or they convey conception with the phrase "to make a baby" (*kodomo ga dekiru*). Many synonyms focus on the physical body of a woman who is great with child, such as the classic-sounding circumlocution "to become heavy-bodied" (*miomo ni naru*) or its informal equivalent "her stomach becomes big" (*onaka ga okiku naru*). The mental state of the pregnant woman and those around her is emphasized by the phrase "a happy occasion occurs" (*omedeta ni naru*), which refers especially to marriage, pregnancy, or birth.

ofukuro Honorable Bags お 袋

Call an English speaker a "bag" (*fukuro*), and she'll be furious at
the implication that she is an ugly girl or a gossipy old shrew,
but Japanese women usually just keep smiling when they hear the
literal equivalent. "Honorable bag" (*ofukuro*) is the affectionate
name sons use when talking informally about their own mothers.
It is considered a humble term, although from the Kamakura
period until the Edo period it was a title of respect for aristocratic
mothers. Today a Japanese son also might call his mom *ofukuro-
san* to her face, adding the polite suffix to show respect to the
woman who traditionally ranked higher than a wife in a man's
heart. This word might sound rude if girls used it, so they rarely
do. The main exception is when they enthuse over the joys of
home-cooked meals, often described as "the taste of the honorable
bag" (*ofukuro no aji*). Restaurant owners like to display this pun-
gent phrase to whet customers' appetites.

Scholars don't know for sure why a mother would be called a
bag, but they've come up with some creative theories. The basis
may be anatomical. If people think their mother's main accomplishment was giving birth, then identifying her with the baglike
form of her womb is almost inevitable. Another hypothesis stems
from the second role women played in traditional Japan, that of
household manager. They were not only in charge of the bags for
storing clothes and utensils, but they also kept a tight rein on the
purse strings of the moneybag. Women retain these responsibil-
ities in contemporary Japan, so they could still aptly be called
"Honorable Moneybags."

Today's most common Japanese word for mother is *okaasan*,
the term preferred by upper-class children in the late Edo period.
It joined the vernacular in the early twentieth century after ap-
pearing in a government-approved textbook. The postwar import
"mama" caught on as a fad, but many new mothers today encourage their kids to use the traditional name. People who do say
"mama" usually leave the term behind with their childhood toys.
Most Japanese adults say *okaasan* or the more intimate *okaachan*
when speaking to their mothers. As they mature, kids also figure
out that they should humbly describe her to others as *haha*, an
alternate pronunciation used when the respectful *o-* prefix and

-*san* suffix are removed from the character for "mother." Japanese strip the trappings from the names of all their kin in this way.

The motherly ideogram is formed by adding two dots for breasts to a variation of the "woman" (*onna*) character. Her vital role in Japanese culture is suggested by the fact that the "mother" figure is used as a component in the characters for "every" (*goto*), "ocean" (*umi*), and "thumb" (*bo*). She joins other characters in such compound words as "mother-sound" (*boin*), meaning vowel; "mother-country-language" (*bokokugo*), meaning native language; and "separate-mother" (*bunbo*), meaning denominator.

These words reflect a culture where the strongest psychological bond is between mother and child, not between spouses, for marriage has long been viewed as a primarily economic relationship. Fathers, who typically are less involved in child care, do not develop the intense interconnection with their children that they have with their own mothers. Traditionally, oldest sons stayed at the family homestead to inherit it, creating a "till death do us part" situation with their mothers. Nowadays weekly magazines exaggerate the theme with "true confessions" about incest between mothers and their adolescent sons.

Wives looking at how the traditional mother-son dynamic lingers in the present tend to complain about their husbands' "mother complex," abbreviated as *mazakon*. Men with such complexes are notorious as the type nobody wants to marry. Meek and weak, these guys can't even resist talking about their mother on dates. After marriage, they take their mom's side against their wife on everything from the day's menu to the question of aborting the fetus in the wife's womb. Women whose husbands suffer from this complex tend to drown their marital disappointment in hopes and dreams for their offspring. Their devotion can cause the cycle to repeat itself in the little one who coos and cries to her, "*Okaasan!*"

sato-gaeri Homecoming   里 帰 り

When a woman is about to give birth to her first baby, it is time for her homecoming (*sato-gaeri*), Japanese style. A new bride in traditional Japan used to be expected to leave her own family behind and move in with her husband's clan. Whenever she made a return (*kaeri*) to her hometown (*sato*) it was a special occasion called *sato-gaeri*. With the exception of apprentices and emigrants, *sato-gaeri* cannot be done by men or unmarried women because, at least in some psychological sense, they have never left their hometowns. The *sato-gaeri* ceremonial visit served to confirm the marriage, so most brides made their first, brief homecoming visit on the third or fifth day after the wedding. Later, when they were enormously pregnant with their first baby, they left their husband behind and returned again to give birth and learn infant care under the wing of their own mother.

Many expectant mothers and fathers in contemporary Japan still want the woman's mother to guide her through the birthing process. Now as in olden times, staying with her own parents also lets the new mother relax to the fullest, freeing her from the responsibility of looking after her husband. Far from feeling left out, the new father generally welcomes the fact that both wife and baby will be cared for by someone with experience in such matters. It continues to be common for women to return to their hometowns for birth followed by a month of recuperation. For subsequent births, the pregnant woman often stays put while her mother comes to look after the pregnant daughter and grandchildren.

Babies used to be born in small buildings constructed for that purpose, called "birth huts" (*san-goya* or *ubuya*). In some villages in Fukui Prefecture, women continued to give birth in these huts until around 1965. When a woman's time was at hand, she was likely to be attended not only by her mother, but also by other female relatives and neighbors, as well as the midwife, who was called a "birth granny" (*sanba*). This intimate community of experienced child-bearers would provide encouragement, advice, and massages for the woman in labor, which is called "battle-pain" (*jintsu*), written with a character (*jin*) usually used in military contexts. Women were expected to endure this pain silently. After the birth, the assistants cut the umbilical cord and washed the baby. Men were absolutely forbidden to enter. One other presence was welcomed to the birth hut in order to safeguard the delivery: the birth god (*ubugami*), the only deity who is considered immune to pollution from birth-related blood. Japanese tradition says birth, like menstruation, is unclean and can pollute people associated with it. Therefore, a new mother usually remained in the hut for two to four weeks, while family and friends brought delicacies to help her regain her strength. The first meal after delivery was offered to the birth god, who stays on the scene to protect the newborn.

Today the setting has shifted to hospitals for the debut of almost all Japanese babies, but some traditional aspects remain. Labor rooms are communal, and women are expected to keep quiet through delivery without anesthetics, though not all succeed. To lessen the pain, at least one hospital recommends repeating the phrase "for the sake of the baby" (*akachan no tame*).

The medical experts surrounding the woman in labor may be female, as in olden days. The 1980 census found that women comprised one hundred percent of Japan's trained midwives, whose official job title has been updated to "birth-helping ladies" (*josanpu*). Female doctors often specialize as obstetricians (*sankai*). Now that male obstetricians have broken the taboo against men's participation, a few fathers are also getting into the act. The Lamaze method, in which men help their wives use breathing techniques and exercises to ease labor pains, is gaining popularity in Japan.

Men as well as women also can give birth in a figurative sense. Birth is a central metaphor for production and creation in the Japanese language. There are two Japanese verbs for giving birth: *osan o suru*, which is strictly for childbirth, and *umu*, which indicates giving birth to anything, from a baby to a machine to interest on a savings account. Industry is written as "birth-business" (*sangyo*), products are "birth-things" (*sanbutsu*), and Japanese-made cars are said to be "Japan-born" (*Nihonsan*).

shikyu   Children's Palaces   子宮

Children's palaces are everywhere in Japan. Neither amusement parks nor ancient nurseries for samurai offspring, these "palaces" are vital elements that every woman in Japan carries with her at all times. *Shikyu*, literally "child's palace," is the most common word for uterus. The quaint fragrance of this term tends to obscure the underlying implication that the womb does not belong to the woman herself, but to her children, real or potential. Her uterus is called a child's palace whether or not she has ever born a baby. The word also crops up in a familiar phrase that implies women are emotional and governed by instinct: "Women think with the uterus" (*Onna wa shikyu de kangaeru*).

The concept that a woman does not have control over her own body is expressed in an adage that states "The womb is a borrowed thing" (*Hara wa karimono*). *Hara* is a vaguer word that can also mean simply "guts." This was not simply a clever turn of phrase, but a description of fact. Feudal law decreed the head of the family should have a son to carry on the family line, whether by a wife or another woman who sometimes was paid for her services. Because the family merely "borrowed" the womb of the mother, her social rank did not affect the child's status, which was determined solely by the father. Japanese no longer think of women as a lending library of wombs, but bearing children is still considered virtually essential to being a woman. A woman's existence can be overshadowed even now by a fetus stirring within her child's palace, at least to the point that department stores display maternity clothes near the children's section, not with women's wear as in the United States.

Although a child's status was once set by the father, men are rarely praised or condemned for the type of babies they sire. This shows in a large set of womb-based nouns that lack male equivalents. For example, mothers who give birth only to girls are "female wombs" (*onna-bara*), while those with all-male progeny are "male wombs" (*otoko-bara*). Neither gets the approval given to a mother of a mixed bag of girls and boys. Tradition also says mothers are responsible for the birth of twins, which was considered unlucky. Mothers were blamed for causing the "misfortune" by such disgraceful acts as making love over the seam of a tatami mat, eating a two-branched turnip, or cutting vegetables on the lid of a saucepan. In some areas, mothers of twins were shunned, while their fathers escaped blame. An even worse type of uterus to have is the "beast womb" (*chikusho-bara*). Women who bear three or more babies at once are called by this beastly word, apparently because folk wisdom says only animals have multiple births. Mothers of girl-boy twins suffer the same appellation. The English equivalent "beast" lacks the profane power of *chikusho*, which is often muttered at those trying times when English speakers would bark, "Damn!"

A mother cuddling her child provides what the Japanese call "skinship" (*sukinshippu*). It means intimate association, especially the touching of skin to skin that results from mother-child kinship, the relationship specified in dictionary definitions. Popular usage is much broader, embracing young lovers who demand more skinship from their partners. This English-like word fills a gap in the Japanese language. Traditionally, Japanese snuggled, hugged, and kissed not as a means of communication, but only for sexual arousal. The usage was reflected in the erotic connotations of verbs for touching. Even in these days of skinship, Japanese above age ten rarely get caressed—or even touched. Adults do not greet relatives with hugs or strangers with handshakes, but meet everybody with a bow.

Skinship in Japan takes some forms that are as unfamiliar to most English speakers as the word itself. Japanese mothers are like koalas, carrying their young piggyback long after birth. They provide skinship all day long by strapping babies onto their backs and lugging them around the house or on shopping trips in an action called "carrying" (*onbu*). The simple *onbu* sling combines the functions of baby buggy, playpen, and rocking cradle all in one. Mother and child move in this symbiotic state for about two years after birth. In winter, an *onbu* cape helps both mom and babe keep warm. These tentlike garments are extended maternity dresses, designed especially for the piggyback pair. The mother and child share not only body heat, but psychological warmth as well. *Onbu* has been cited as one source of the passivity and dependence that characterize Japanese society, because babies grow up virtually immobilized, always encountering the world as a tiny spectator through mama's comforting mediation.

Skinship with a baby doesn't end when it's taken from the *onbu* sling for meals, bath, or bed. Breastfeeding is common. Some hospitals don't even allow new mothers to give their newborn a bottle of cow's milk or any other "artificial nutrition" (*jinko eiyo*). Nurses insist that they should at least try suckling the babies on "mother's milk" (*bonyu*) for as long as they are in the hospital. Major hotels and department stores go out of their way to accommodate nursing mothers by equipping women's restrooms with chairs for nursing in comfort and tables for changing diapers. Building designers thus take into consideration the reality of a new mother's life: She can rarely go out without her baby, yet she is too modest to breast-feed in public.

Many Japanese children sleep in the same room with their mothers until they are about ten years old, though some parents nowadays try to provide their children with their own rooms. There is also a word "co-sleep" (*soine*) for sleeping right beside a baby, or lying beside the child until it sleeps, although other usages are possible. A proverb advises parents to "Sleep in the form of a river" (*Kawa no ji ni neru*), referring to the "river" ideogram that consists of a short line resting between two long strokes, like a child between parents. If it comes to a choice of sleeping with the baby or the man, women sometimes pick the little one who has snuggled on her back all day. This does not necessarily seem unnatural to today's fathers, who were yesterday's piggyback papooses. Men almost never use their greater physical power to carry infants around, but when a second child is born, the father has been known to move with the older one into separate sleeping quarters so that no one need sleep alone.

The father is most likely to get his share of parental intimacy while bathing, a prime example of skinship. The Japanese think of the bath as a place for communication, an intensified version of the camaraderie that joins people washing dishes side by side. Scrubbing and soaking together is a time-honored custom for all friends and family, especially children and their fathers. Many Japanese girls bathe with their dads until puberty, while boys and fathers may continue sharing the tub for a lifetime.

---

umazume Stone Women   石 女

Stones are cold, hard, and lifeless. The Japanese language implies that women who cannot bear children are the same way. The word *umazume* ("stone woman") or just *umazu* means a woman who is infertile, what an English speaker might call barren. It can also be written with characters that spell "no-life woman" or "non-birthing woman." *Umazume* is one of the worst words in the entire Japanese language. Many people under thirty-five don't even say it, although they acknowledge its power over them. If they hear *umazume*, it reverberates with the despair of medieval women who were divorced for not bearing children. According to superstition, the presence of a stone woman could make a whole village wither. As if the shame they endured in this world were not bad enough, the souls of infertile women were said to fall into "stone women's hell" (*umazu no jigoku*), where they were forced to dig up bamboo roots with lamp wicks as a torture. Today many Japanese still can't help feeling something is wrong with childless older couples.

Surveys have shown that all but one to three percent of Japanese women want to give birth. The vital importance of fertility to the Japanese is also revealed by many wedding traditions. For example, a type of seaweed called *konbu* is included among the gifts exchanged by families at betrothal time because it sounds somewhat like "bearing a child" (*ko o umu*) and "to rejoice" (*yorokobu*). Women's value has long been measured by their fertility, no doubt because it is so obvious and so essential. This was especially true back when child mortality rates were high.

Sadly, the hard times endured by a good many stone women were based solely on their choice of men. Sterile men in Japan have escaped being scorned with words as stone-cold as *umazume*. Recently, as both science and communication among women progress, the language has given birth to terms for men such as *inpo* (short for "impotent") and *tanenashi* ("seedless").

Ancient infertility cures focused on the woman. Depending on the region where she lived, she would be advised to try sleeping in the bedroom of a couple with children, or stepping over a placenta. Concerned friends might slip into her sleeve a pebble that had been offered by a new mother to the birth god (*ubugami*). Traditional attitudes continue to skew infertility research and treatment by the Japanese medical establishment. Artificial insemination, often a remedy for a husband's sterility, is easier, cheaper, and more likely to succeed than the female infertility cures that result in so-called test-tube babies. In most countries, artificial insemination is more popular, too. However, Japanese hospitals vied to set up facilities for creating test-tube babies in the mid-1980s, while only one major clinic offered artificial insemination.

Sterilization, officially termed "eugenic surgery" (*yusei shu-jutsu*), is much less common in Japan than in other industrialized nations, especially for men. Although male sterilization is simpler, about three-quarters of Japan's sterilizations are undergone by women, more than double the ratio in the United States and Britain.

5

Office Flowers Bloom
WORK OUTSIDE THE HOME

danjo koyo kikai kinto ho
Equal Employment Opportunity Law 　　　　　男女雇用機会均等法

Working conditions in modern Japan have been as different as
night and day for female and male. The legally mandated differences, called privileges by some and rights by others, were swept
away in 1986 when the Equal Employment Opportunity Law
(*danjo koyo kikai kinto ho*) took effect. Although the Japanese
Constitution guarantees equality of the sexes, previous legislation
allowed only men to labor between 10:00 P.M. and 5:00 A.M.,
except for women working in the rare jobs deemed both feminine
and essential, such as actress, nurse, telephone operator, and stew-
ardess. Women were forbidden to work underground or at twenty-
six jobs considered too dangerous, such as handling heavy objects
and cleaning power transmitters. By eliminating these and other
gender-based differentials and issuing fine words in favor of equality,
the new act aims to close the wide gap between wages received
by women and men in Japan. However, the equal employment
law lacks teeth; there are no penalties for violators. The relatively
tough proposed bill was watered down by political compromise,
as was the key word in its title. The commonly used English
translation remains "equal," but the original term *byodo* was
replaced by *kinto*, whose meaning comes closer to parity than to
equality.

Menstruation leave (*seiri kyuka*) is probably the most unusual
benefit to be eliminated. Only South Korea and Indonesia still
offer it. Such leave originated with the Japanese, who first granted
it to members of an all-women volunteer work corps during
World War II. The practice of allowing a few days off to men-
struating women each month became law in 1947. This institutionalized system did not inspire women to celebrate their biological
rhythms. Rather, most Japanese women felt too embarrassed to
request the leave. Men in the 1980s began joking that they would
take time off for *seiri kyuka*, too. *Seiri*, a euphemism for menstruation that literally means "physiology," can be pronounced
the same way but written differently to mean putting things in
order. The man who takes a masculine *seiri kyuka* works at a far-
flung branch office apart from his family. Once or twice a month,
he gets permission to trek home for a visit. He arrives with

suitcases full of dirty underwear and sweaty socks, which he passes on to his wife. She gets them in order for him to carry back when his leave is over.

Some employers used to say it was impossible to promote women because the law prescribed different working conditions for them. This is among a multitude of factors that made Japan one of the few countries where the wage gap between women and men grew in the 1970s and early 1980s. A study by the Organization for Economic Cooperation and Development found that Japan was the only one of eleven industrialized nations where the hourly wage gap grew for manufacturing work. The average Japanese woman earned forty-nine percent of a man's wage in 1982, compared to fifty-three percent in 1971. Over this same period, many more Japanese women took jobs, especially low-paid part-time jobs that brought the average down. Another important factor was women's tendency to quit their jobs upon marriage or childbirth, sometimes due to pressure from their bosses. So they missed out on the automatic raises that come with seniority. This became a vicious circle when women resigned because their chances for promotion were slim. Discriminatory hiring practices meant that women gravitated toward low-paid industries and small companies, which are also known for their small wage scales.

Even before the new law was passed, women were finding greater opportunities by working for foreign companies in Japan or in new facets of the information and service sector, where physical strength is not essential. Some started their own companies to provide ingenious services that run the gamut from finding temporary meeting rooms to placing wake-up calls for single young executives. The fact that a large number of women are in these fields becomes a magnet for more, especially when a female president does the hiring. Many men disdain these jobs because they tend to be with small companies or on a free-lance basis.

The question of women's wages has assumed greater importance now that the female work force has swelled to over a third of Japan's total employed population. There are more than four times as many wage-earning women as there were in 1950. The reasons for the trend are numerous. First, women have more time for employment due to longer life spans, lower birth rates, and more labor-saving devices in the home. Women's educational level has risen, as have their aspirations to independence. Their financial needs are growing, too, as housing prices rise faster than inflation. Some of these same causes lie behind the fact that more married women are seeking employment. Among working women, the marital status ratio has reversed from two-thirds single in 1962 to two-thirds married in 1984. Working wives and their working husbands lead a lifestyle called "both working" (*tomo-bataraki*).

It will be years before the full impact of the Equal Employment Opportunity Law is known, but personnel officers of Japanese companies quickly flocked to seminars on how the law affects them. A 1985 Kyodo News Service poll of two hundred Japanese companies found thirty-five percent planned to introduce sexual equality in recruitment, employment opportunities, promotion, and loan financing. The rest were about evenly split between uncertainty and the belief that their work places were already egalitarian.

geisha   Arts People   芸者

Geisha means "arts person." As the word implies, it is love of the arts that often prompts contemporary women to become *geisha*, a lifelong career demanding study of classical dance, the lutelike shamisen, and several singing styles. Unlike most other segments of Japan's entertainment business, the *geisha* world allows women to work steadily until they become old and gray, for the emphasis is on artistry and conversational virtuosity over looks. Japanese generally respect *geisha* as preservers of cultural traditions, although some prejudice exists because their love affairs frequently fall outside marriage. Female art-lovers who lack the commitment to become a *geisha* probably never will glimpse one, however, since their expensive services are almost exclusively aimed at and bought by male politicians and businessmen. *Geisha* generally do not sell sexual favors, though they used to entertain prostitutes and their guests in the bygone licensed prostitution quarters. Laws in the feudalistic Edo period explicitly prohibited them from offering anything more intimate than art. It is said that a *geisha* can now earn more than a typical salaried worker on her wages and tips alone, so she is not forced to sell her body as sometimes happened in the past. Still, many do find patrons for a free-flowing exchange of sex, money, and love.

The financial picture was much more grim for *geisha* of the past. The profession originated in the Edo period, and the earliest recorded use of the term *geisha* was made in Kyoto in 1751. The first *geisha* were male, but the field was gradually taken over by women, who had been working since the twelfth century as professional dancers called *shira-byoshi* (white rhythm). Before the modern age, most *geisha* were the daughters of either other *geisha* or families so poor that they were forced to indenture their girls to *geisha* houses. The girls usually began their service before age twelve by doing household drudgery and then rose through the apprentice ranks to become full-fledged arts people in their mid-to-late teens. The only way they could escape their debt, which sometimes continued to grow as they kept up their costly wardrobes, was if a patron bought their freedom.

Improved conditions for contemporary women in all walks of life have helped make *geisha* a vanishing species. Even the poorest families would not consider indenturing a daughter now. Due to child labor laws and compulsory education, contemporary girls don't begin *geisha* training until beyond the age when they used to finish their apprenticeship. Some skip that phase altogether and launch their careers in their twenties. Nationwide, only about seventeen thousand *geisha* remain, far fewer than the eighty thousand who graced Japan in the 1920s. Their numbers declined as Japan mobilized for war, and by the 1940s, *geisha* were forbidden to all but the military elite.

Today their role in providing feminine companionship and conversation is being taken over by the women sometimes derided as "artless arts-people" (*gei no nai geisha*). *Hosutesu* (hostess) is the most common word for the women whose job is to chat, dance, and sing with men drinking in bars. Becoming a hostess is much easier than becoming a *geisha* because musical training and expensive kimonos are not required. Customers also find these women in Western dress more in tune with the times. Most are middle-class women who chose their job for its high wages. Both hostesses and *geisha* sometimes save up to become the *mama-san*, or managers, of their own bars, a job more common for women in Japan than for those in the West. A male bar manager is a master (*masutaa*), and a waiter is a boy (*boi*); the word *papa-san* is reserved for the *mama-san*'s patron. While the mamas and the masters now take the low-status route to success, the *geisha* have become recognized as true arts people maintaining traditions of the past.

gyosho no obasan   Street-Peddling Aunties   行商の小母さん

Women commonly called "street-peddling aunties" (*gyosho no obasan*) scuttle through modern Japanese cities like misplaced turtles beneath the weight of bundles as big as themselves. Written with the characters for "little mother," *obasan* is applied to any middle-aged woman in the same way that Americans use "auntie." It also sounds just like the word for a blood-related aunt. Another, less common word for the street peddlers is *katsugiya*, literally "shoulder-burden peddler," which can also refer to people who carry a bundle of superstitions in their mind. These women bring remembrance of humanity's enormous capacity to survive hardship and, more importantly from their perspective, they bring vegetables. In the Tokyo area, they journey six days a week from the countryside to sell produce in the neighborhoods of the central city. They used to grow the crops themselves, too, but now many buy them from neighboring farmers. Some remain bent over even after they have laid out their vegetables for inspection, as if another load were still weighing them down. Some are widowed, some not. Some are middle-aged, others so ancient that customers talking with them stretch their *obasan* into *obaasan*, changing "auntie" to "granny."

It's rare to see a man in this line of work, partly because agriculture has become a largely female trade in Japan. In 1980, women comprised sixty-two percent of the farm labor force, and more than a fifth of them were age sixty or over. Postwar economic growth and labor-saving machines that enable women to do more have caused many farm men to commute to urban jobs, or to move to the city for a few months of seasonal employment, or to forsake agricultural work altogether. The result is called "triple-dear agriculture" (*sanchan nogyo*), or farming done by granny dear, grandpa dear, and mama dear. Wives are the main-stay of Japanese agriculture now, but urban job opportunities for women have started to pull them away, too. Few young women long to devote their lives to the often grueling labor of a farm woman, epitomized so dramatically by the bent-over vegetable peddlers.

hobo to kangofu
Sustaining Moms and Watchful Protectresses   保母と看護婦

Nurses and nursery school attendants are occupations so domi-nated by women that the female gender is built into the job titles. Only recently have a few men joined their ranks, bringing with them new titles that don't deny their masculinity.

Child-care workers at nursery schools are called *hobo*, a com-pound meaning roughly "sustaining mother." The younger the student, the more likely the teacher will be female. In 1980, forty-three percent of all teachers were women, but they were concen-trated in early childhood education to the tune of ninety-nine percent of nursery school attendants. There was no need for a male-oriented title until the 1970s when men began entering the field and asking to be called "sustaining father" (*hofu*). A series of legal reforms in the late 1970s opened national day-care ex-aminations and training schools to men, who were referred to as *hofu* in the amended law. Now some sustaining fathers and moth-ers are advocating an all-purpose title, child-care workers (*hoiku-sha*).

In a similar way, nurses are "watchful, protecting ladies" (*kan-gofu*). Sixty-nine percent of all medical practitioners were female in 1980, yet all but three percent of nurses were women. The new minority of men in nursing has asked to be called "watchful, protecting gentlemen" (*kangoshi*). Medicine is generally consid-ered a nurturing occupation, appropriate for women, so it was the first professional career opened to them in modern times. Starting in 1884, women were allowed to take the national licens-ing exam in medical arts, and Japan's first medical school for women opened in 1900. Female doctors and college teachers were Japan's pioneering professional women.

When a Japanese woman gave birth, it used to mean giving up any job outside the home, too. Now it is coming to mean child-care (*ikuji*) benefits for the growing number who decide to nurse along their jobs as well as their babies. Public opinion is also shifting in favor of working mothers.

The mingling of motherhood and employment is made possible by a law that guarantees mothers the right to fourteen weeks of maternity leave. Until 1986, this leave lasted twelve weeks. The leave is split into pre-natal (*sanzen*) and post-natal (*sango*) periods. Bosses can decide whether or not to continue the woman's wages during this time. Upon submission of a medical certificate, an expecting or new mother can obtain a transfer to a less taxing job. Employers are prohibited from firing the woman during maternity leave or for thirty days thereafter. The law also suggests (but does not require) that companies provide "child-care leave" (*ikuji kyugyo*) after the maternity leave expires. To set a good example, the government grants a one-year child-care leave to female teachers, nurses, and nursery school attendants who work in public institutions. As of 1981, fourteen percent of Japanese companies and other organizations had followed suit. In reality, many Japanese mothers say they still feel coerced into quitting their jobs when they give birth.

If they succumb to the corporate pressure, they will never be able to take advantage of the nursing breaks that look so nice on paper. Women in Japan are legally granted two 30-minute breaks daily for the first year after giving birth as "child-care time" (*ikuji jikan*), a benefit taken by about a third of employed new mothers. The law leaves employers free to decide whether the nursing breaks will be paid or unpaid leave. *Ikuji jikan* sometimes is loosely translated as "nursing breaks." In days gone by, most mothers used their breaks to breast-feed their infants. However, today many women slice their "nursing break" time from the start and finish of their work day and use it to deliver and retrieve their little ones from day-care centers.

The Japanese government calculated in 1982 that nursery schools had room for about a fifth of Japanese children up to age five, roughly equal to demand. It was still hard to find child care for periods longer than eight hours, at night, in remote rural areas, or for handicapped children. In the early 1980s, women working at night often resorted to the crowded, unsanitary facilities called "baby hotels" (*bebii hoteru*). A government crackdown on child-care licensing succeeded in closing many of the dangerous baby hotels. As a result, there were only twenty-four regulated night nurseries in the entire country in 1986.

Fathers may not be able to breast-feed their offspring, but they're well qualified to be day-care center chauffeurs—and some want this responsibility. Since about 1980, cries of sexual discrimination have arisen from the male side of the labor force. Men have organized coalitions that agitate to achieve child-care rights.

Men do not get an automatic leave when their babies are born, but becoming a father has its own rewards at work as well as at home. Employees' monthly salaries are comprised of basic pay plus allowances to reimburse them for such burdens as overtime work, job responsibility, and dependents at home. Family allowances are granted to the person designated as the head of the household, usually a man. Thus, when a woman gives birth, her husband may get rewarded with a raise in salary to help support the newly arrived bundle of joy.

joryu   Female Stream   女 流

Joryu, literally "female stream or style," is tied like a silly bow onto perfectly sound job titles when a woman does work that Japanese tradition assigns to men. The resulting words make a frivolous impression, such as *joryu sakka* (authoress), *joryu gaka* (lady artist), and *joryu bungaku* (ladies' literature). The label is most often used in the arts, where it implies not only female, but feminine in the stereotyped meek-and-mild sense. Therefore, some in the female stream prefer words such as "woman author" (*josei sakka*) if their gender must be specified.

At times, the *ryu* is dropped when forming compound words for women who cross into traditionally masculine lines of work—for example, "woman doctor" (*joi*) or "female teacher" (*jokyoshi*). The less respectful pronunciation *onna* is applied to such occupations as pickpocket (*onna suri*) and thief (*onna dorobo*). Then there are the "lady journalists" (*fujin kisha*) and "lady police officers" (*fujin keisatsukan*). These and countless words like them separate women's activities from the mainstream because gender is not specified when men hold the same positions, and there is no equivalent term "male stream." Linguistically speaking, Japanese in many jobs are assumed male unless labeled female.

Government statistics from 1980 confirm how rare it is for Japanese women to enter certain fields. Women accounted for only 6 percent of scientific researchers, 3 percent of accountants and tax administrators, and 2 percent of public officials. In the "female stream" of the arts, women comprised 26 percent of artists, designers, and photographers, and 18 percent of literary writers, journalists, and editors.

The ratio of women working as religious leaders in 1980 was 18 percent. Shamanesses (*miko*) have practiced in Japan since the dawn of civilization. In modern times, several Shinto sects had female founders (*onna kyoso*). Christianity also was quick to accept female leadership in Japan. Women have been admitted to Japan's Protestant clergy since 1941, longer than in many Western nations, partly due to the wartime shortage of men.

Jobs as guards and soldiers are among the last to open to women. Except for nurses, women were not allowed to join the Ground Self Defense Force until 1967. A shortage of willing men convinced the air and sea forces to start recruiting both sexes for regular duty several years later. Nowadays, women comprise about one percent of Japan's military personnel. The doors of the Maritime Safety Academy, Aeronautical Security College, and Meteorological College were opened to women in 1979. Since then, access has also been granted to the exams for aviation controllers, national tax specialists, Imperial Palace guards, immigration guards, and prison officers. The first women to take on these and other jobs, from jockey to orchestra conductor, are heralded in the mass media as exotic wonders.

What is arguably the nation's most important job remains legally reserved for men. Six women reigned as empresses in the seventh and eighth centuries. Since then, women have been forbidden to take the imperial throne and rule as empress, literally "woman emperor" (*nyotei* or *jotei*), with two notable exceptions in the Edo period. Throughout history, they have, however, been allowed to serve as empress in the sense of emperor's wife (*kogo*).

Like monogrammed initials dressing up a plain sweater, OL is applied to one of Japan's more humdrum jobs. OL (*o-eru*) stands for "office lady," as accurate a description as any for their vaguely secretarial duties. The OL is the butt of many jokes, but few people stop to consider how the nation's business would probably screech to a halt without OLs to do paperwork and field phone calls. Such basic duties comprise the jobs of many OLs.

Office ladyship is the most common job for Japanese women today. OLs of all ages make up about a third of the female labor force. The OL boom began as offices expanded after World War II. At first the female office worker was dubbed a BG (*bii-jii*), a snappy acronym for "business girl," or so the Japanese thought. They decided that title was no longer OK when they discovered that many English speakers already used "B-girl" for "bar girl," a type better known as a prostitute. The editors of *Josei Jishin*, a women's magazine, came to the rescue of their readership and launched a search for a new name that was more ladylike. OL was chosen in 1963 from the suggestions mailed in by their readers.

Japan also has a multitude of OGs (*o-jii*), who are not, as one might imagine, "office gentlemen." There is no such animal. OLs become OGs when they visit their alma maters to remember their salad days. Current students welcome back alumni of both sexes, greeting them as OGs and OBs (*o-bii*), "old girls" and "old boys."

---

paato   Part-time Jobs   パ ー ト

What the Japanese call part-time jobs (*paato*) would be full-time in the eyes of many Westerners. Japanese law defines "part-time" as up to thirty-five hours weekly. But with the addition of over-time, many female part-time employees work the equivalent of full-time. Because they are classified as part-timers, they still receive far lower wages and fewer benefits than the men and (increasingly) women hired for "full-time regular" jobs.

In everyday conversation, part-time jobs in Japan go by different names depending not on the type of work, but on the type of worker. When college students earn extra money at jobs like frying noodles or flipping hamburgers, people usually say they have an *arubaito*, a term borrowed from the German, meat-and-potatoes word for work. When a married woman takes a side job, it generally goes by the incomplete-sounding name *paato*, or "part," an abbreviation of the English "part-time." The word first appeared in Japan in a 1954 advertisement for a department store recruiting saleswomen. Thirty years later, the majority of female part-timers work in sales or service industries, and more than three-quarters are past age thirty-five. Their legions are rapidly growing. Female part-timers numbered three million in 1983 and accounted for more than twenty percent of employed women, a sharp increase from nine percent in 1960.

Companies give their part-timers only a tiny share of their resources, which enables the part-timers to do likewise. Women flock to these jobs because they don't want to devote all their energies to a company. Compared to full-timers, they have much more freedom to set their own hours, take days off, leave work-related worries at the job site, and resign when they feel like it.

The tax structure is another reason why Japanese women, as well as their husbands, accept the low wages for female part-timers. As long as a wife earns less than 900,000 yen ($6,000) per year, her income is not taxed and her husband can still take advantage of the 570,000 yen ($3,800) spouse deduction allowance. If her earnings surpass the limit, she will have to earn *a lot* more in order to offset the tax increase.

On a larger scale, Japanese society depends on female part-timers to be the safety valve in Japan's famous lifetime employment system. Part-timers are often laid off in recession with short notice and no retirement benefits, at least until recently. Japanese newspaper editorials hailed the "first significant step taken for the benefit of part-timers" in 1985 when some laid-off part-timers complained to their mayor in Settsu City of Osaka Prefecture, resulting in a new municipal "mutual aid system" to provide an allowance equal to about forty-five hours' pay to people who retire after completing one year on a *paato*.

Another pressure valve is provided by women laboring part-time in their homes. Instead of being called *paato*, this low-paid, female-dominated cottage industry is known as "inside employment" (*naishoku*). The term originated in feudal times, when it was applied to the side jobs of samurai. In 1983, over a million females did piecework at home, from sewing on buttons to cutting electrical wires; they comprised ninety-three percent of home workers. Their typical work day was 5 hours 48 minutes, and for their efforts, they earned slightly more than half the hourly wage of a part-timer.

shokuba no hana   Office Flowers   職場の花

"Office flowers" (*shokuba no hana*), like Japanese female employees in general, are characterized by their short-lived blossoming. The "office flower" is not a plant, but an ornamental variety of "office lady" (*o-eru*). A woman of any age can be an office lady, while office flowers must be young enough to serve as decorations for brightening and softening the predominantly masculine office environment. Responsibility may fall on the shoulders of an office lady, but an office flower would never be burdened with duties heavier than serving tea, making copies, or answering the phone. Such tasks are often referred to simply as "serving tea" (*ochakumi*).

All but the heartiest of office flowers wither in a few years, but even the ones who don't resign their jobs are usually replaced with new "flowers" before they start to droop in their late twenties. The fate of the wilting office flower is sometimes an "office marriage" (*shokuba kekkon*), a term for marriage between people who meet on the job. Such matches are even promoted by some companies because managers want male employees to spend their time working, not dating. From management's viewpoint, retired office flowers make especially good wives because they are more sympathetic to the pressures their husbands face at work.

Government statistics show that length of employment is brief for all female wage earners, young or old, in the office or out. Jobs with the shortest tenure are called *koshikake*. Usually it denotes a chair—the unpadded kind comfortable only for temporarily "hanging your hips," as *koshikake* literally means. Young women say they seek these positions so they can "study society" for a few years before they get on with the serious business of raising a family. At present, job tenure for Japanese women averages 6.5 years in all industries, a momentary flowering when compared to the male "life-time employment" model.

Many managers still expect females to settle into jobs after they finish school, then vacate them when they enter into marriage, which is also known as "eternal employment" (*eikyu shushoku*) for women. Such conservatives consider the latest possible deadline for a woman's retirement to be the birth of her first child. However, a landmark judicial decision declaring compulsory retirement upon marriage to be unconstitutional was handed down in 1966. A stream of judgments since then has continued to discourage employers from treating their female staff like a bouquet of flowers to be replaced at the first sign of age.

6

Pillow Talk
SEXUALITY

chikan Molesting Fools 痴漢

Women squeeze onto Japan's jam-packed trains with a tingle of anxiety similar to what females the world over feel on dark, lonely city streets. Crowded trains are the most common scene of encounters with "foolish men" (*chikan*) who fondle the thighs, buttocks, and breasts of women pressed helplessly against them. The word reflects the indulgent way these fools are viewed by society in general. Women usually save their complaints for when they're alone with their own gender.

More than horror stories, strategy is what the women discuss. The sardine-can crowding of the trains makes escape impossible. Many women admit they do nothing more than slink away in misery at the next stop, for fear of retaliation or being followed home. Kicking, punching, and stabbing with a nail carried for that purpose can all be effective, as is waiting for the next stop and then dragging the offender off to the authorities. Shouting releases the victim's anger, but also invites scrutiny at an embarrassing moment.

Women's tendency to feel ashamed for being victimized continues to be reinforced. An example emerged at the 1985 Tsukuba Science Exposition, where the female guides, called "companions" (*konpanion*), were trained to respond to *chikan* in the crowds. When a man's hand slithered toward her crotch, each guide was told to say "I'm so sorry!" as if she had accidentally bumped into his hand.

gokan Rape 強姦

The word *gokan*, meaning rape, is itself an assault on women's sensibilities. The word consists of the ideogram for "coerce" followed by a character built of three women (*kan*). Meaning wickedness or seduction, *kan* is probably the character most widely recognized as discriminatory. It also can be pronounced *kashimashii* to express the milder evil of noisiness. The composition of *gokan* calls to mind the twisted reasoning that rape victims are guilty of "asking for it."

Japanese law defines rape as sexual relations with a female by use of force or intimidation without her consent. Marital rape was first recognized by a Japanese court in 1986. Any man who has intercourse with a girl under age thirteen is guilty of rape, even if she has agreed. Rape is punishable by two years' to life imprisonment.

Like the act itself, the Japanese term for rape arouses strong, sometimes conflicting emotions. Few women use the word, partly because it is so graphic, and also because some hope to eradicate the *kan* character. It is already on the road to extinction for it has been banned from the company of some two thousand general-use characters approved for use in newspapers. Press reportage accordingly uses the vaguer word *boko* (assault) or turns to English for a term—*reipu*—that sounds neutral to Japanese ears.

While they applaud the quashing of the sexist character, feminists do want the public to recognize the problem. Rape victims often tend to keep quiet because they are stigmatized and suspected of provoking the attack. The women who opened Asia's first Rape Relief Center (*Gokan Kyuen Sentaa*) in Tokyo in 1983 believe only about five percent of rapes are reported to police. Figures compiled by Japanese police show the rate of rapes reported per 100,000 inhabitants nationwide declined slightly in 1982 to 2, in contrast to a rate of 34 in the United States during the same year.

junketsu kyoiku   Purity Education   純潔教育

Japanese celebrate happy times in their lives by eating rice made flavorful and pink through cooking with red *azuki* beans. For some of the nation's women, this mellow feast marks their first formal sex education lesson. Until recent years, girls were not always told about the changes in their pubescent bodies until their first menstrual period prompted a flow of frightened questions. Then their mothers set the red beans and rice to boiling and sat down to explain how babies are made. Although the boys in the family were not told the cause of the celebration, the festive rice reassured the woman-child that her shocking developments were natural and good. Today this comforting rite of passage is dying out, especially in the cities. Centuries ago, the initial sex education lesson was sometimes supplemented shortly before a woman married, when she received a scroll of graphically erotic pictures showing her what to expect on her honeymoon night. These collector's items go by such poetic names as "spring pictures" (*shunga*) and "pillow pictures" (*makura-e*).

In the first half of this century, sex education came to be called "purity education" (*junketsu kyoiku*), a double-speak term still used fondly by a few older conservatives. As the word suggests, they believe the main reason for teaching about sex is to condemn it outside the purifying sanctity of marriage—especially for women. Purity education was abandoned officially decades ago in favor of "sex education" (*sei kyoiku*), but the topic remains almost untouched in the Japanese education system. The first sex-related lesson in the national curriculum guidelines in the mid-1980s was about physical changes accompanying puberty, to be taught in fifth grade. Usually teachers separate girls and boys before broaching the subject. The guidelines recommend teaching a bit about hormones in junior high, followed by more esoteric anatomical data in some high school health and science classes. However, each school is left to decide for itself whether to follow the guidelines, and sexuality is still such a touchy subject in Japan that parents dread discussing it and different teachers approach it very differently. Those who teach high school health classes are almost always physical education instructors whose primary interest is sports.

In contrast to the sterile silence surrounding children at school, the mass media provides a blitz of sex information that is too often inaccurate and sexist. Overall, Japanese children seem to be finding out about sex at progressively younger ages, probably due to the lewd content of television, magazines, and comic books. Erotic comic books for adults are openly read on crowded Tokyo trains, giving children ample exposure to these dubious learning tools. Sex on prime-time television in Japan has extended even to children's programming such as the now notorious (and canceled) 1980s cartoon "Machiko, the Give-In Teacher" (*Maitchingu Machiko Sensei*). *Maitchingu* is a nonsense word created by blending the English "-ing" suffix with an expression for surrender, *maitta*. Every week Machiko, a beautiful, unmarried elementary school teacher, squealed with delight as she gave in to her male students' attempts to feel her breasts and buttocks.

As the number of teenagers having abortions rises, some teachers are making efforts to supplement the meager offerings of sex information traditionally available at school. In the all-female environment of the home economics classroom, for example, younger teachers have begun discussing sexuality in the context of human relationships.

kai Shellfish   貝

Long ago the Japanese decided shellfish (*kai*) satisfied both empty stomachs and minds hungry for an appropriate symbol of female genitalia. This image appears most dramatically in Japanese fertility festivals where gigantic representations of vaginas or penises are paraded down streets lined with happy revelers. One such spring festival, honoring female anatomy, is held in Inuyama, Aichi Prefecture, where a huge model clamshell is carried through the streets, opening and closing gently in the breeze. A little girl tucked inside tosses rice cakes to the crowds. The sexy shellfish is supposed to grant marital bliss, babies, cures for sexual diseases, and bounteous crops.

As Japan continues to industrialize, fertility rites are losing their importance, but the shellfish imagery continues to thrive when men discuss the opposite sex. *Awabi* (abalone), *shiofuki* (spraying surf clam), and *shijimi* (corbicula) have all been used to refer to women's genitals. Depending on her particular endowments, a woman's vagina may be likened to a sea anemone (*isoginchaku*) or said to have a bumpy "ceiling of herring roe" (*kazunoko no tenjo*).

Shellfish are but one of the incredibly varied images Japanese use for this sensitive topic. Another set of terms likens the vagina to a container (*utsuwa*), or perhaps a fine vase (*meiki*). In ancient times, it was a homonym meaning fiery place, hollow place, or excellent gate (*hoto*), a pronunciation still in use today but written with the character for "yin," the female element that is dark, passive, and negative. It was called a tea cannister (*ochatsubo*) or simply tea (*ocha*) in the Edo period, when tea was a rare luxury longed for by the masses in the same way men may thirst for a woman's body.

Even Kannon, the Buddhist Goddess of Mercy, is called into

service as a symbol of female anatomy. Kannon is one of the most popular bodhisattvas in Japan because cries for help are so real to her that she not only hears but even "sees the sounds," as her name literally means. She has the ability to assume any form, female or male, depending on her worshippers. Scholars continue to speculate over why, when, and how this male deity in India was transformed into a being almost always depicted as female in Japan. Although priests and educated people consider Kannon male, most Japanese still pray to her as a goddess. She has been worshipped in Japan since about the seventh century, especially by women who call to her for reassurance and help during childbirth. There is a peculiar logic in the fact that men who cry out for sexual thrills sometimes say they are going to worship Kannon when they visit a strip show, using the deity with strong female associations as a euphemism for female genitals.

The textbook terms for vagina (*chitsu*) and clitoris (*inkaku*, literally "hidden kernel") are neither as common nor as crude as the word that men most often apply to female genitals. *Manko*, derived from the characters for "absolute place," is similar to "cunt" in its vulgarity. The absence of terms females feel comfortable using indicates that they seldom discuss their sexuality among themselves. If they do mention it, they might refer to the "secret place" (*hisho*) or just "down there" (*asoko*). The more colorful Japanese euphemisms may sound whimsical to Western ears, but they provoke the same negative feelings in many Japanese women that English-speaking women might feel when they hear words such as "pussy"—a velvety sweet word that bares its claws when used in a sexual context.

There is no agreed-upon cute word for a girl's genitals as there is for a little boy's *ochinchin*, although some families make up their own terms such as "the honorable importance" (*odaiji*). Several years ago, some Japanese feminists noticed the inequality and tried to rectify it by creating a new term that means something like "dear slit" (*wareme-chan*). *Wareme*, or crevice, another common vulgarism for vagina, is dressed up with the diminutive ending *-chan*. The nickname has been slow to catch on. Some women have adopted a positive and slightly humorous new term from the title of a popular women's magazine. They refer to their genitals as "woman herself" (*josei jishin*).

A man who goes to visit Number Two isn't settling for second best. He's off to see the woman who rates first in his heart, since she's his mistress in an extramarital love affair. *Nigo* (Number Two), sometimes followed by the polite ending *-san*, is a slightly old-fashioned Japanese term for a woman to whom a husband turns when Mrs. Number One is home with the kids. Actually, Mrs. Number Two is probably home with another set of kids, because this word does not apply to a brief infatuation or a tryst with a prostitute. Like the English speaker's "kept woman," the *nigo* is virtually a simultaneous second wife, staying home with the children of the man whom she loves and who loves her back, complete with financial support. "Second wife" implies remarriage in English, but these dual family commitments exist simultaneously in Japan. One explanation for this arrangement is that a man's original wife is sometimes chosen for him by his elders, while his heart arranges the second union.

Such an undertaking is expensive, and popular wisdom says the men most likely to indulge in these affairs are politicians and others with wealth to spare, who may also keep a Number Three and Number Four on hand. Not everyone approves of adultery, so the word *nigo* is whispered behind people's backs and never used as a form of address. To some people, however, dallying with many mistresses is something of a status symbol because to do it, a man must be not only rich, but also resourceful, energetic, and determined. It is often said that "having a concubine is a male's medal" (*mekake o motsu no wa otoko no kunsho*).

Marital relations were not always so. In ancient Japan they were flexible; as late as the Heian period, both women and men entered into fairly permanent liaisons without renouncing other potential mates. The nobility of both genders often had several spouses in a lifetime, although men still tended to be more polygamous. Women were restrained by the fact that their children would be social failures unless they were claimed by a man from another household of equal rank. The Chinese idea of ranking these wives and concubines was adopted between the eleventh and fifteenth centuries. Indeed, the word *mekake* (concubine) did not exist until the fourteenth century. It comes from the expression "to hang the eyes on" (*me o kakeru*), meaning to catch someone's eye or to look after someone. During the feudalistic Edo period, a woman could be executed for adultery, while a man was free to keep a harem under a single roof, with the first wife in charge of one or more concubines, or to set up his women in separate homes and flit back and forth. Legal reforms of the late nineteenth century continued to support concubinage by stipulating that wives must accept as their own any of their husband's *shoshi*. These were illegitimate children whose father recognized them by giving notice to a registrar.

From this situation, where men had so many more chances to philander, springs the still-popular belief that women are the jealous sex. Today's Japanese bride wears a hat called a "horn-hider" (*tsuno kakushi*) at her wedding to show she will curb this fault, which supposedly is apt to poke like sharp devil's horns from any woman's head. For a woman to show jealousy is "to grow horns" (*tsuno o dasu*), a term derived from a recurring plot in Japanese dramas: the transformation of a jealous woman's spirit into a demon.

Reality partially contradicts this. Japanese women's usual reaction to their husbands' extramarital affairs is benign neglect. It is not unheard of for a wife to go so far as to stick a pack of condoms in her spouse's suitcase before he departs for an overseas "business" trip. Such women say they are protecting their marriage from disruption as well as disease. Sex outside marriage tends to be regarded as harmless as long as the husband pays for it with money, not love. But jealous horns may sprout if a husband keeps a *nigo* sweetheart. Wives sum up their attitude in words that are heard less frequently now that many hope for faithful husbands: "The floating heart is fine, but the true heart is off-limits" (*Uwaki wa ii, honki wa dame*).

Floating heart means adultery. The assumption that infidelity is a male preserve shows in the word *jonan* (woman troubles), which implies pity for the guys lured into trouble by seductive women. There is no comparable term for "man troubles." In fact, the idea of troublesome women is so deeply imbedded that it has become a stock phrase among Japanese fortunetellers, who can tell from a mole or a twist of the eyebrow that fate has cursed a man with the "mark of woman troubles" (*jonan no so*).

Similarly, *nigo* denotes only female paramours, although the word itself does not specify gender. A unisex term is "lover" (*aijin*). Built from the characters for "carnal-love person," *aijin* sounds immoral, secret, and dark in comparison to "romantic-love person" (*koibito*), which applies to young sweethearts. To put love affairs in crude terms, a woman can be referred to—in gesture or word—as a "little finger" (*koyubi*), while a man is the "parent finger" or thumb (*oyayubi*).

Linguistic barriers have not kept Japanese wives from having illicit lovers. Surveys have trouble measuring the extent of their infidelity and how it compares to their husbands' behavior. Recently, a Kyodo News study found 2.5 percent of wives and 20 percent of husbands had been unfaithful in the previous year, whether with a lover or a common prostitute, while a magazine called *21* reported that 26 percent of housewives and 56 percent of working wives had tried extramarital sex.

rezubian Lesbians   レズビアン

Lesbians in Japan are at a loss for words. They find unacceptably insulting or voyeuristic nuances in almost every Japanese term for homosexual women. They make few efforts to reclaim these slurs, the way American lesbians have embraced the word "dyke," or to invent new words in their native tongue. Rather, identifying themselves with the Greek island of Lesbos, where love between women flourished in the seventh century B.C., they call themselves *rezubian* (lesbian). People sometimes abbreviate this term as the more derogatory *rezu*.

The major sources of lesbian words lie outside the gay community. Japanese pornography provided "shellfish combo" (*kai awase*) and "plover" (*chidori*), which offend at least some of the women they label. Mental health specialists, who tend to think of homosexuality as a disease, say *doseiai*, literally "same-sex love." Homophobic people jeer at lesbians as "honorable pans" (*onabe*), a play on the slang "honorable pots" (*okama*) for gay men. These terms liken the differing shapes of the anus and vagina to pots and pans.

The existence of Japanese lesbians has long been discounted. A linguistic example of this oversight is a pair of traditional terms:

"male charms" (*nanshoku*) for erotic love between men and "female charms" (*joshoku*) for heterosexual love. Lesbians are left out. Still, double dildos and other sex toys of pre-industrial times speak irrefutably about the existence of lesbians. Lovemaking between women was also a motif in Japanese erotic art at least as far back as the nineteenth century.

Today's lesbians leave their mark on Japan through their own journals, organizations, and bars. Gay bars usually cater to men, with such notable exceptions as the colorfully named Space Dyke, which bloomed briefly in the mid-1980s. The nation's first International Lesbian Conference was held in 1985. However, most Japanese lesbians are still deep in the closet, a state so expected that there is no Japanese phrase for hiding one's homosexuality.

Life in the closet usually includes masculine and feminine role playing, except among feminists who strive to overcome gender stereotypes. The Japanese "femme" is called *neko* (cat) or *nenne* (ingenue). The "butch" is *otachi*, from the Kabuki term for leading actor (*tachiyaku*). Japanese lesbians lack a verb for coming out of the closet, though a few, modifying the English phrase, do say *kamu auto suru*.

seiko   Mixing Heart and Life   性 交

A loving, wholesome attitude toward sexuality is shown in the "sex" character developed ages ago. "Sex" (*sei*) is written in Japanese by combining the ideograms for "heart" and "life." It is followed by the character for "mixing or exchanging" (*ko*) in the word for sexual intercourse (*seiko*). This suggests the open expression of the heart's desires by the living body, a meaning that may not be entirely accurate. Evidence that sex often fails to warm women's hearts comes from an extensive survey on Japanese female sexual behavior and attitudes conducted by the editors of *MORE*, a popular women's magazine.

When *The MORE Report on Female Sexuality* was published in book form in 1983, many Japanese women hailed it as the biggest and best study of their sexuality to date. The survey of 5,770 Japanese women revealed that most women desire sex but do not initiate it, and that seventy percent have pretended to reach orgasm. As a 42-year-old housewife explained to the researchers,

"Faking orgasm is the woman's role. It's a psychological reward for my husband's efforts to battle our enemies in the outside world." Ironically, previous generations of Japanese women felt duty-bound to hide their orgasms.

The proper term *seiko* is about as rare in everyday talk as "Hey, let's engage in sexual intercourse." In making such a proposition, Japanese might turn to their own pop songs or movies for such famous come-ons as "Let's drink coffee together at daybreak" (*Yoake no kohii o issho ni nomo*) or "How about it? Don't you feel like getting sweaty with me?" (*Do da? Ore to ase kaku ki wa nai ka?*).

Some of the common synonyms for intercourse come from English, so they echo exotically in Japanese minds while striking native speakers hard and fast: "do sex" (*sekkusu suru*) and "get in bed" (*beddo-in suru*). The all-purpose verb *suru* is combined with the nonsense phrase *nyan-nyan* for a cute expression that even the most modest young woman would feel comfortable saying. "Sleep" (*neru*) is a common synonym in both languages, and Japanese has its own version of "going all the way": literally, "to cross the line" (*issen o koeru*). They can also "knot the relationship" (*kankei o musubu*). "Making love" has no literal equivalent, although people adopt verbs such as "to love each other" (*aishiau*) for this context. The euphemism "to do something good" (*ii koto o suru*) suggests a positive attitude toward sex, while men's tendency to brag about their exploits shows in a slang word virtually never said by women: "the real performance" (*honban*). This term is usually used in screen and stage circles to denote the difference between a mere rehearsal and the actual performance before a live audience or camera.

Since women tend to play the passive role, some sex terms have evolved with the strong implication of who is doing it to whom. "To put a hand on" (*te o tsukeru*) can mean to demand sex, transmitting the image, in one Japanese woman's words, of "a man imprinting himself on a vulnerable woman through a sexual relationship." The word for hand (*te*) comes in handy as an indirect way of talking about all stages leading up to and including intercourse, generally with the connotation that the hand is male. An "unhandled" (*teirazu*) person is a female virgin. The handling begins when a man "holds out his hand" (*te o dasu*) by asking her for a date or sex. If he doesn't hesitate to make an approach and speeds through the preliminaries to get right down to intercourse, his "hand is fast" (*te ga hayai*). If she refuses, he may resort to rape, which can be rendered with the characters for "to ram a hand into" (*tegome ni suru*). This ramrod of a term is seldom used today, except in historical novels and movies that re-create feudalistic Japan.

Literature provides words for intercourse that are the most poetic, though the least often voiced. Lovers "exchange pillows" (*makura o kawasu*) or "exchange feelings" (*jo o kawasu*), using a verb form of the *ko* in *seiko*. When they do it again, they begin to "pile up pillows" (*makura o kasaneru*). As in English, their bedtime conversation is "pillow talk" (*makura monogatari*). Extinct verbal forms of "pillow" (such as *maku* or *makuraku*) are used to recount various people's pillowings in the literature of the Nara and Heian periods.

shojo   Home Girls   処女

Double standards tarnish virginity in Japan. First, Japanese virgins are divided into two categories, female (*shojo*) and male (*dotei*). Both are fairly positive terms conveying innocence, but *shojo* curtsies her way into many more discussions aside from the topics of sex and marriage. *Shojo*, literally "female in the home," is compounded with other words to denote purity or beginning, as with the English "maiden voyage" or "virgin wool." The Japanese language contains a full spectrum of these words, including *shojo saku* for a writer's first published work and *shojo tocho* for the first ascent of an unclimbed mountain. Never is *shojo* replaced by the male equivalent *dotei*, which combines the ideogram for "child" (*do*) with the one for "chastity" or "fidelity" (*tei*).

The same character begins the word *teiso*, which means virginity before marriage and fidelity thereafter. Japanese dictionaries define it as something only women do, lending credence to the classic double standard: Many Japanese men still hope to marry virgins, but have no intention of "saving themselves" for their chaste wives. A 1986 survey of young men by *With* women's magazine showed how slowly morals are changing. Only 44 percent said it was OK for an unmarried woman to have sex—*if* she loved the guy. (An unromantic 4 percent said the sooner she lost her virginity, the better.) The sole inquiry about masculine virginity concerned the age at which the respondents had lost it, and all had, though 68 percent had never married. However, the men's wish to wed a virgin may not come true; a government report shows Japanese girls are sampling sex at ever younger ages. Some try to repair the damage by going to a doctor for "maidenhead regeneration" (*shojomaku saisei*), a twenty-minute operation in which the remnants of the hymen are sewn together or partially reconstructed with plastic.

Another sign that virginity is more important for women than for men in Japan is that *dotei* stands almost alone as one of a handful of words for male virgins, while *shojo* dwells among a large harem of synonyms. The most general and widespread term is *shojo* itself, the expression even doctors use. The more romantic mood of "maiden" comes from *otome*, which is also the translation of the Virgo zodiac sign. It originally meant young female. A word that comes up in literature and the conversation of older people is *kimusume*, which combines the ideogram for "daughter" with one meaning pure. Then there are cruder words used by men with a prurient interest in females who are "new" (*sara*). Despite this rich vocabulary, Japanese borrowed yet again from English to obtain *baajin*. This Japanized English word is used when the speaker desires a synonym free of embarrassing connotations, as well as in certain set phrases like Virgin Mary (*Baajin Maria*) or "virgin road" (*baajin rodo*), a common term for the main aisle of a church on wedding day. Because virginity is so closely tied to women in Japan, it follows that giving it up also becomes a greater loss to them. They become "damaged goods" (*kizumono*).

---

sopu redi   Soap Ladies   ソープレディ

Neither side is truly talking turkey in one of the most recent Japanese efforts to clean up the image of the women who are now supposed to be called "soap ladies" (*sopu redi*) instead of "Turkish-bath girls" (*torukojo*). These are two of the newest expressions for possibly Japan's most doubletalked-about phenomenon, the prostitute. Japanese scholars count more than thirty synonyms for prostitute, but not a single word to describe the men who buy their services.

The latest whitewash campaign began in 1984 after a Turkish diplomat stationed in Japan became incensed by the gaudy brothels that masqueraded as bathhouses under his country's name. Officially, a soap lady's job is to make bubbles and rub down her customer, and sometimes that is all that happens. But it is common knowledge that soap ladies do perform sex for pay behind closed doors at Turkish baths, which are most concentrated in the same areas formerly set aside for licensed prostitution. The Turk took his complaint to the government and the press, spurring establishments from Osaka to Yokohama to yank down their offending neon signs. An estimated twenty thousand women nationwide were renamed "soap ladies," at least by members of the Tokyo Special Bathhouses Association, which picked the neat new name as the winner of a euphemism contest that drew 2,200 entries. Their work place is now termed "soapland," prompting some people to call them by the less ladylike name "soapland girls" (*sopurandojo*). No objections were raised by the soap industry, but feminists bubbled angrily that a better solution would be a crackdown on the organized crime syndicates behind the dirty business.

Prostitution was legal in Japan until the late 1950s, when a new law forbad the business that the Japanese government had been officially regulating for eight hundred years. Some scholars figure the nation's first prostitutes were Shinto shamanesses (*miko*) or the vassal women (*uneme*) sent to the capital by their families in order to cement political alliances. This practice dates back at least to the sixth century.

The government got into the act about six hundred years thereafter when the first brothels sprang up. As early as 1193, the ruler of Kamakura appointed officials to supervise the activities of ancient playboys who paid for their pleasures. Literally translated, the word for the women they bought was "playgirls" (*yujo*). Girls from poor families, indentured by their parents on contracts lasting ten or twenty years, had no hope of escape except the slim chance that a patron would pay the "pillow fee" (*makura-gane*) to buy their freedom. Society tended to view them with more pity than blame because obedience to parents was considered a greater virtue than personal chastity.

During the Edo period, many of the playmates were herded into a network of at least twenty-five officially licensed quarters, though unlicensed districts remained. Yoshiwara in present-day Tokyo was the most famous play center, inspiring the vivid woodblock prints of the courtesans and actors peopling its *ukiyo*, a word that has homonyms meaning either "floating world" or "sad world." In the term *ukiyo*, the Buddhist idea of existence as sorrow is combined with a Chinese word evoking the transience of life.

As Japan industrialized in the late nineteenth century, impoverished peasant girls began to be sold into sexual slavery outside Japan. Such a girl was called "Miss Foreign-Bound" (*karayuki-san*). The first Japanese female exchange students, five girls aged six to fifteen, were sent to America and Europe in 1871, around the same time that other Japanese women began to see the world as sexual slaves from Shanghai to Sausalito. The number of *karayuki-san* peaked in the early twentieth century. As many as a hundred thousand foreign-bound misses were sent abroad before the government banned the traffic in prostitutes in 1920. Living conditions were so harsh that most of them died in foreign lands before they turned thirty.

The brothel system within Japan also grew bigger and more organized with industrialization. By 1930, more than fifty thousand prostitutes were divided into 511 licensed quarters. The Japanese military also recruited "comfort ladies" (*ianfu*) to console Japanese soldiers in war zones during World War II. The "comfort" they supplied was sex. The comfort ladies are said to have numbered more than a hundred thousand, with eighty percent being Korean teenagers, and the rest Chinese or Japanese. They usually worked twelve hours a day, spending less than half an hour with each man.

This concept did not end with the war. Less than a week after Japan surrendered, the Tokyo Metropolitan Police Headquarters began gathering women into the licensed quarters with pleas that they needed to protect the purity of respectable Japanese women by making sure the American troops got enough "comfort." Backed by government funding and propaganda about sex-starved

U.S. soldiers, the comfort-lady population in Japan swelled to as many as seventy thousand.

Japanese women gained the vote in a 1945 postwar reform package, and at least partly to please them, the Diet outlawed this long-standing institution in 1956. That law, still in effect, focuses on punishing brothel organization and public advertisement of prostitution, rather than on the act itself, which continues under various new names. The tendency to idealize prostitution shows even in the standard term used in the law forbidding it. The activity banned is "selling spring" (*baishun*).

One way to get around the law is to take a sex tour to a less wealthy Asian country, such as Korea or Taiwan. Another, increasingly common tactic is to visit a different sort of prostitute that has emerged in Japan. Typically, Thai and Philippine women are lured there with promises of lucrative jobs as singers and dancers. After arrival, their passports are taken by gangsters who force them into prostitution. Like the "Miss Foreign-Bound" of old, these women journey overseas to sell their bodies, so they have been dubbed "Miss Japan-Bound" (*Japayuki-san*). More than eighty-five percent of the roughly five thousand aliens arrested for violating the terms of their visas in Japan in 1984 were hostesses and strippers. Another new entrant into the prostitution business is the Japanese female university student, whose combination of a student's part-time job (*arubaito*) with "selling spring" (*baishun*) has been condensed into the slang *arubaishun*, or part-time prostitution.

sukin redi Skin Ladies   スキンレディ

"Skin ladies" trudge from door to door, combing Japan for housewives who will buy the intimately useful product called "skin" in Japanese slang or, more properly in either language, "condom" (*kondomu*). One favorite brand of condom is Skinless Skins, source of the slang term. When asked about the word *sukin redi*, most Japanese say they don't know what to call these door-to-door condom peddlers, and they don't care to know. Their squeamish attitude is exactly why skin ladies are so successful, controlling as much as forty percent of the condom market in the mid-1980s.

Cloistered housewives are often too self-conscious to buy in public.

The market is massive, for Japan is said to have the world's highest condom use rate. The *Mainichi* newspaper's National Opinion Survey on Family Planning showed that condoms are used by more than eighty percent of Japanese married couples who practice contraception (*hinin*). The next most popular method is rhythm, at twenty-three percent, and the two techniques are often combined. In contrast, usage of the Pill remains strikingly low because Japanese law still deems it unsafe except for regulating menstruation, and doctors are reluctant to prescribe it unless there is a pressing need.

Women, being the sex that gets pregnant, naturally feel more urgency than men about preventing unwanted conceptions. In Japan, they turn to condoms. Japanese men do sometimes buy condoms at drugstores or street-side vending machines, but "skins" are considered primarily a women's product. Japanese condoms are snuggled right up against the tampons in supermarkets. Women's magazines are also the preferred advertising medium among condom makers.

The manufacturers also invest a lot in their skin ladies, paying them commissions of thirty to fifty percent and rewarding the sales champs with free vacation trips. Most are middle-aged married women with kids, the trustworthy type whose opinions on family affairs seem unimpeachable. These upstanding citizens are lured into Japan's own version of the skin trade by the good wages, higher than most jobs open to women, including door-to-door sales of other products. The money compensates them for both the social stigma and, more importantly, the dangers of their line of work. Husbands are usually away when they come knocking, but the skin ladies fear that a man may answer the door and, aroused by the merchandise, attempt a rape. Accordingly, they usually ask a friend to wait nearby, ready to intervene if the skin lady doesn't check in regularly.

The customers tend to be so embarrassed about birth control that they gladly pay higher prices to avoid being seen purchasing in public. Moreover, they don't want to endure the encounter with the skin lady any more often than necessary. So they buy a one- or two-year supply of big, economically priced "family packs" of condoms. A few are said to be so desperate to end the disconcerting sales pitch once and for all that they buy more than enough condoms for a lifetime.

yugurezoku   The Twilight Tribe   夕暮族

Japanese slang sheds a softly romantic light on couples where the man is decades older than his mate. These middle-aged Romeos— or any older men worthy of flattery—were usually called "romantically gray" (*romansu guree*) starting at the end of World War II. The term has been easing into retirement since 1979, when a prize-winning novel on the theme came along with the alluring title *Yugure Made* (Until Twilight).

"Twilight tribe" (*yugurezoku*) caught on quickly as the new term for couples consisting of a man aged 45 to 55 with a woman, 21 to 23. Author Junnosuke Yoshiyuki portrayed just such a pair in his novel, but the phenomenon is no fiction. Japanese women in general profess much interest in men old enough to have a wealth of gray hair—and a matching abundance of money. Aging executives are often spotted guiding their young mistresses to pay-by-the-hour inns. They may well be coming from their place of employment, where she serves tea and does light secretarial work. Such liaisons are so common that there is a special term for them: "office love" (*ofisu rabu*). This is not to be confused with romances sparked between unmarried office colleagues of roughly the same age, which tend to conclude in "office marriage" (*shokuba kekkon*). A shadow of immorality falls over the twilight tribe, for middle-aged Japanese men are almost invariably married, and not about to change it.

The oldster in these twilight pairs is always male. In the rare instance where the reverse occurs, it is again the man, and not the romantically gray woman, who is bestowed with a lyrical name. A man younger than his lover is called a "young swallow" (*wakai tsubame*).

7

Nice Middies Do
AGING

Japanese women no longer pass directly from middle age to old age. A new life phase was inserted between the two traditional age brackets in the late nineteenth century by Japanese studying German medicine. They created the term *konenki* to refer to the stage that English speakers call menopause. Literally "renewal time," *konenki* has implications beyond just the end of menstruation, which can be specified with the more technical term *heikei*. "Renewal time" is closer in nuance to "the change of life": a long, gradual transition from the late thirties or early forties to the late fifties. Japanese women say that reaching renewal time means irritability, depression, dizziness, difficulty in concentrating, loss of energy, weakening eyesight and hearing, gray hair, and—most upsetting for Japanese women—an inability to suppress feelings. The depression may stem from ambivalence about menopause. While glad to be free from the monthly inconvenience and the worry of possible pregnancy, many women fear the loss of their health, sex appeal, and value as women. The link with femininity is made explicit in the colloquial expression for menopause "to become a man" (*otoko ni naru*).

Although Japanese traditionally celebrated the start of menstruation, its end has not inspired similar ceremonies, nor even a specific word. Before *konenki* was coined, the problems associated with menopause generally were considered part of the "path of blood" (*chi no michi*). This term for gynecological disorders dates back at least to the tenth century. Meanwhile, Japanese specialists in Chinese medicine blamed menopausal troubles on "stale blood" (*oketsu*). Both these concepts were supplanted by the newer *konenki*.

The "renewal" character in *konenki* sounds a hopeful note, but the word has a negative nuance and is frequently followed by "obstacles" (*shogai*). Japan's public and medical establishment alike commonly assert that women living the modern life of ease feel more menopausal symptoms because they dwell on themselves too much, though the facts tend to disprove this.

One trouble that rarely plagues Japanese women at menopause is hot flashes. In fact, there is no Japanese word for this complaint, which Western doctors have long assumed to be a universal symptom of the change of life.

mibojin   The Not-Yet-Dead People   未 亡 人

When a woman's husband dies in Japan, she begins to be called a "not-yet-dead person" (*mibojin*). She may also think of herself this way, for the word is said to have originated among widows. It is a rather formal term, used in such phrases as "war widow" (*senso mibojin*). Many Japanese use "not-yet-dead person" unconscious of its literal meaning, but the original implication was that once a woman's husband is dead, she has outlived her purpose and has nothing left to do but await death herself.

A more informal term for widow is "after-family" (*goke*), as if her whole family succumbed with her husband. Men, however, are never "after-family." *Yamome* comes closer to being a unisex term for people who outlive their spouses, but actually there are several *yamome*, homonyms with different spellings. A female *yamome* is written either with a chilling character that combines "woman" and "frost," or with another character that joins "division" and "house." In recent years, this has become the preferred character for official references to widows. The character for male *yamome* originally denoted a large fish. Widowers are said to grieve day and night, never getting a wink of sleep, until their ever-open eyes resemble a fish's. To avoid confusion in conversation, people tend to specify widowers as *otoko* (male) *yamome*.

Clearly, husbands are expected to expire first in Japan. And they usually do. The average life expectancy in 1985 was 80.5 years for females and 74.8 for males, the world's longest life spans. Since men usually marry younger wives, the typical woman can look forward to more than five years of not-yet-deadness. Indeed, it is considered so unnatural for a wife to precede her husband in death that the superstitious say bad luck will befall the man who goes to his own wife's cremation ceremony, although women usually attend when their husband is cremated.

Widows in the Edo period faced some unique legal restrictions. They were bound by law to wear mourning garb for thirteen months, more than four times longer than a widower's requirement. Some showed their determination to remain faithful to dead husbands by tying their hair in the ponytail style (*kirisage*) of widows. To remarry, they needed their in-laws' permission.

The widow's lot is no longer as desperate as it once was. Companies pay the husband's pension to the not-yet-dead person, though only a fraction of what it would be if he were alive. Widows' problems were eased a bit more in 1981, when a revised law granted women half of their husband's estate, with the rest split by their children. Previously, the widow's share was one third. Now so many widows succeed their husband as the president of the family business that Japan has more female company presidents than female managers.

Today as yesterday, few of the not-yet-dead folk remarry. Middle-aged and elderly men still tend to propose to younger women looking for their first husband. In a way, remarriage may be more imperative for Japanese men, since most of them rely on their wives to cook and to maintain their household and wardrobe. The disastrous results of this role division are epitomized by the proverb "Widows bear flowers, widowers breed maggots" (*Onna yamome ni hana ga saku, otoko yamome ni uji ga waku*). In other words, losing a wife results in squalor, while losing a husband frees a woman to make herself more attractive—supposedly in an effort to land yet another man who needs her care.

naisu midi   Nice Middies   ナイスミデイ

Advertisers had to invent a nice Japanese term for middle-aged women: "nice middies" (*naisu midi*). It became a household word in the mid-1980s, thanks to ads for Japanese National Railway. JNR workers figured out that men aren't the only ones who enjoy, and can afford to buy, a weekend away from the spouse and kids, so in 1983 they created the nice middy pass for group travel by women thirty and over. The following year, 34,500 middies were nice enough to buy the discounted train fare.

Each year the nice middy pass is promoted with a new slogan such as the jubilant theme for 1985, "Women take off!" Posters everywhere pictured exactly the type of fun that appeals to these women: A trio of friends in carefree cotton kimonos sit before a feast of sashimi and saké at a Japanese-style inn, probably with its own hot spring. They laugh conspiratorially, like schoolgirls who cut class to romp in the real world. One is even pouring her own beer, shocking in a culture where keeping other people's glasses full is paramount and where many women are only beginning to indulge in alcohol—again, largely at the urging of advertisers.

Middle age sets in early in Japan, especially for women. Some Japanese still look to ancient superstition and see the turning point as the unluckiest of the various "unlucky years" (*yakudoshi*): age thirty-three for women and forty-two for men. Women are generally thought to hit their prime, literally "female flourishing" (*onna-zakari*) in their twenties or thirties, but a man's prime (*otoko-zakari*) falls in his forties or fifties when his career is at its height.

Another reason middle age seems to pounce earlier in Japan is that people there died much younger in the not-so-distant past. The typical Japanese woman didn't live more than half a century before 1950; now the average life span surpasses eighty. Slowly but surely, this reality is pushing back the definition of middle age. *Toshima*, a derogatory term for older females, referred to those in their twenties in the Edo period, but now it is applied to women in their thirties.

One theory says *toshima*, literally "years added," originated in the licensed prostitution quarters of old, where females passed their "prime" in their twenties to become *toshima* who served as waitresses and housekeepers. In general, the words for mature women in Japan have been fewer and less complimentary than terms for younger women. The value placed on female youth is summed up in the proverb "Wives and tatami mats are better when new" (*Nyobo to tatami wa atarashii ho ga yoi*).

The term most commonly applied to middle-aged women is *obasan*, which is similar to the English "ma'am" in usage and feeling. Though a homonym of the word for "aunt," it is written as "little mother." One minor crisis point in the life of a Japanese woman is the day when strangers start addressing her as Little Mother. The venerable term is easiest to take from youngsters, but can become an insult in the mouths of one's peers. The Japanese woman knows she really looks old when people lengthen the *a* into the similar-sounding *obaasan*, which means grandmother.

Obaasan are so elderly that their skin has become lined with row upon row of wrinkles, one following another like the waves of the sea. That is one explanation of the Japanese word *obaasan*, in which the ideograms for "woman" and "wave" join to compose another character that means grandmother. Male wrinkles seem to have attracted less attention, for no wave dampens the word for grandfather, *ojiisan*. Both terms can also refer to the elderly in general. Less commonly heard synonyms include "ancestor mother" (*sobo*), used to refer humbly to one's own grandmothers, and *rojo*, which denotes an old woman without hinting at her reproductive history.

The prefix *o-* and suffix *-san* coat the grandmotherly character *baa* or *baba* with politeness. As in any Japanese form of direct address, other endings convert them into the more intimate names people call their own grandmas. Strip away the trappings and lengthen the final vowel, and the resulting word, *babaa*, means an ugly old hag. When Japanese play cards, the jinx card that Americans call the "old maid" or the "joker" is scorned as the *baba*.

The unadorned *baba* also bobs up in a quip that Japanese women used to make about the qualifications of the ideal husband: "house included, car included, no hag" (*ie tsuki, kaa tsuki, baba nuki*). In Japanese tradition, oldest sons generally came with aging moms, and the bride was expected to join the household to honor and obey the matriarch. As that family system disappears, the plea for "no hags" is heard less often. Some women may even wish for a live-in grandma to serve as babysitter (*komori*) while they go out to work or play. The idea of hiring someone outside the family to babysit remains foreign to most Japanese.

About a fifth of Japanese households still weave at least three generations together in a complex and durable tapestry of inter-relationships. Elderly Japanese who live in these extended families say their deep love for their grandchildren is one of the major reasons they like the live-in lifestyle. They delight the youngsters by retelling Japanese fairy tales, and grandchildren return their affection by massaging their elders' aching muscles.

In the old days when most kids grew up sharing a home with

their father's parents, that bond was much tighter than the tie to their maternal grandparents. This situation is suggested by the terms "outside grandchild" (*soto mago*) for the offspring of a daughter who married into another family and "inside grandchild" (*uchi mago*) for those who carry on the family name—almost always the sons' children. In current usage, the definitions are often simplified to children who live with the grandparents, and those who don't. While these distinctions are emphasized by the Japanese language, the sex of the grandchildren is not. There are no single words for granddaughter and grandson, only a unisex character written by joining "child" and "lineage" (*mago*).

The priority given to inside grandchildren is dissolving now that more Japanese live in nuclear family units. Both sets of grandparents are visited, but the women, who do most of the child care, naturally feel more eager to visit their own moms and more relaxed when they are together. The mother's feeling rubs off on her children, who may come to feel closer to the maternal *obaasan*. This tendency is reinforced because women often ask their own mothers to babysit, a favor more difficult to request from a mother-in-law.

obasute-yama　Mount Granny Abandonment　姨捨山

Mount Granny Abandonment (*obasute-yama* or *ubasute-yama*) rises four thousand feet toward the sky in central Japan. It gets its darkly colorful name from ever-popular legends about taking old women to mountaintops and abandoning them to die. Too weak to do much work, a grandmother could become an intolerable drain on her family's food and finances. Not far from the mountain, the makers of *Obasute* saké print their brand name phonetically, avoiding the graphic characters that mean deserting an *uba* (old woman) or an *oba* (which can apply to miscellaneous female relatives).

One variation of the story, said to have been imported from India via China, tells how an old couple's wise advice saves their village after their son defies an order to discard them. The version found in the twelfth-century tale *Konjaku Monogatari* and fifteenth-century Noh play *Obasute* by Zeami chronicles the agony of a man whose wife is urging him to dispose of an aging relative.

This scenario lives on in contemporary Japanese arts, especially the short story "Oak Mountain Song" (*Narayama-bushi ko*) by Shichiro Fukazawa. Feature films based on it were made in 1958, and again in 1983 when the theme helped director Shohei Imamura's movie (*Narayama-bushi ko*) garner the Grand Prix Award at the Cannes International Film Festival.

Scholars looking at the high socioeconomic status of old people in even the poorest Japanese communities surmise that the practice of forsaking old women who couldn't earn their keep was never as common as the many and diverse legends about it. Japanese have been celebrating their senior citizens with special festivals for at least three hundred years. These have evolved into Respect for the Aged Day on September 15, possibly the world's only national holiday on the theme. Individuals are honored by family gatherings and gifts when they turn 60, 70, 77, 88, and 99, although usually men are heaped with more hoopla than women are on these birthdays. Far from trying to hide their age, many elderly Japanese let their gray hairs show and boast of how long they have lived.

The psychological truth behind the granny-abandonment legends is not only the young people's desire to get rid of a burden, but also the elderly woman's own death wish. In Imamura's award-winning film, it is the aged mother who insists that her son must carry her to die peacefully on the snowy mountain peak—and so he does. Today, old people's prayers for a painlessly abrupt death pour into temples specializing in this particular plea.

Sometimes they take matters into their own hands. International statistics compiled by the World Health Organization show elderly Japanese women have an extremely high suicide rate compared to their peers in other countries. Among women aged seventy-five or older in Japan, 5.7 in 10,000 died from self-inflicted injury in 1984. This is below the Japanese male suicide rate in the same age bracket, but much higher than women of the same age in nations such as the United States (0.5 per 10,000), West Germany (2.8 per 10,000), and Hong Kong (3.4 per 10,000).

Legends about abandoning granny, which focus on the conflicts within a single family, could be seen as a microcosm for the problems faced by Japan as a whole. Its population is aging with unprecedented speed. The United Nations predicts that the country's proportion of elderly will double by 2015, when one in five Japanese will be sixty-five or older. The two major reasons are the lengthening of the average lifespan and the falling birth rate. Moreover, an estimated sixty percent of the population over sixty-five is female. Leaving old women to die on mountaintops is out of the question, but in the mid-1980s the Japanese government began considering a plan to export its senior citizens to "Silver Towns" constructed in nations where the cost of living is lower.

shutome   Mothers-in-Law   姑

Placing the "female" ideogram beside the symbol for "old" automatically creates the Japanese word for mother-in-law (pronounced either *shutome* or *shuto*), a powerful position that loomed larger than life in the traditional Japanese family structure. Old age is not as essential for defining a father-in-law (*shuto*), which is written by combining the symbols for "male" and "mortar" (as for grinding a pestle against). Today both terms are most often applied to the husband's parents, but research has shown that in ancient matriarchal times, when a man married into his wife's family, *shuto* used to denote the wife's father. Neither character bears any resemblance to those for mother and father, suggesting that natural parents and in-laws play widely different roles.

Beginning in the eleventh century, marriage in Japan came to mean the woman literally married into her husband's home, where his mother trained the young bride to conform to the family ways. The oldest son was singled out to inherit the entire homestead and bear the responsibility of caring for the parents in their old age. Even today, the vast majority of three-generation households consist of parents and their son's family, though sharing a home with a daughter is becoming more popular. Most of the Japanese elderly live with their children and grandchildren, so mother-in-law conflicts are notorious. Unlike the Western model, where the wife's mother and husband clash, the classic Japanese scenario pits the husband's mother against his wife.

Some skirmishes are expressed in sayings: "Daughter-in-law

and mother-in-law are like dogs and monkeys" (*Yome to shutome, inu to saru*). Japanese know that dogs and monkeys fight like cats and dogs do in the West. "Don't feed autumn eggplant to a daughter-in-law" (*Aki-nasubi yome ni kuwasu na*) is usually interpreted as advising stern discipline for young brides, who would be spoiled by such delicacies as autumn eggplant, though some say the treat must be withheld purely for the sake of the *yome*'s health. Dissatisfied mothers-in-law convinced their sons to divorce so often that there used to be a special term for it, "disposal via mother-in-law" (*shutome-zari*). Lorded over by her *shutome*, the feudal Japanese daughter-in-law was almost a household slave, rising first each morning, doing household drudgery all day, and going to bed last at night. She was also subjected to the whims of her husband's siblings, known as the "little mothers-in-law" (*ko-jutome*) and "little fathers-in-law" (*ko-juto*). The beleaguered young bride naturally dreamed of the day when she would wield the power of a mother-in-law.

The Japanese mother-in-law is no longer in such an enviable position. The young bride is said to dominate the *shutome* now, to the point that many older women prefer to live separately from their sons. Nevertheless, the term for mother-in-law continues to carry enough nuance of tyrannical power that some people avoid it in favor of circumlocutions such as "husband's mom." When discord does erupt, nowadays some families resort to the courts. Almost half of the Japanese husbands who asked courts to mediate family disputes in 1983 cited conflicts between wife and mother as the cause.

Now as in the past, years of living together tend to change the way the *shutome* and her son's wife feel about each other. Traditionally there came a time when the aging mother-in-law was satisfied that the bride could run the household. In some districts, female authority was transferred symbolically when the mother-in-law handed over the wooden paddle (*shamoji*) used to dish out rice at meals. The balance of power tilts further in favor of the younger woman as old age creeps up on the mother-in-law. Finally they switch roles when the bedridden *shutome* is nursed by her daughter-in-law.

sodai gomi　Giant Garbage　粗大ゴミ

People in Japan always sort their garbage into three categories for easier disposal: combustible trash like eggshells, flame-resistant rubbish like beer cans, and last but not least, "giant garbage" (*sodai gomi*), the big, coarse, hard-to-dispose-of junk like broken refrigerators. Or like retired husbands, in the cruel slang of the 1980s.

Women call their own husbands "giant garbage" to complain that they mope aimlessly around the house, good for nothing, always getting in the way. Until they retire from demanding salaried jobs, these *sodai gomi* sorts spend so little time at home that they never develop their own household niche. While wives devote all their energy to the home, husbands define themselves in terms of their jobs, as is revealed by another wifely insult for retirees, who have been stripped of the company name that provided their identity. They are "unlabeled canned goods" (*raberu no nai kanzume*). The extent of this irreverent attitude can be gauged by the letters-to-the-editor column of the *Mainichi* newspaper, where a controversy over the term *sodai gomi* raged through more than sixty letters in 1984. Now younger women are adopting "giant garbage" to complain that pre-retirement husbands don't help around the house during the few hours they spend at home after work.

A word for middle-aged women who worry that their executive husbands will turn into trash upon retirement also joined the Japanese vocabulary in the 1980s. They are said to have entered "the autumn of awareness" (*shishuki*). This is a play on the term for adolescence, which the Japanese poetically call "the springtime of awareness" (*shishunki*). When a wife turns forty, she may begin to feel uneasy not only about how she will cope with a retired mate, but also about her purpose in life once their children have left the nest. The expression for her mid-life crisis was invented by Hayo Kawai, a psychology professor at Kyoto University, then popularized in the mid-1980s by Kyodo News Agency reporter Shigeo Saito with his book *Tsumatachi no Shishuki* (Wives' Autumn of Awareness), a collection of interviews with disillusioned housewives.

Some causes of the *shishuki* phenomenon were also documented in a 1983 government study, which found that overtime work, after-hours entertaining, and long commutes meant only forty-one percent of Japanese salaried men ate dinner at home every night. A third spent less than three waking hours a day with their families. Wives have been known to make a virtue out of necessity by repeating the saying "Husbands should be healthy and absent" (*Teishu wa jobu de rusu ga ii*). The prospect of getting a healthy dose of their husband's presence for the first time fills them with anxiety, especially since Japanese women born before World War II were socialized to expect distant female-male relations within an extended family. In these larger households, women were supposed to wait upon men, and the marital relationship was just one among many that made life fulfilling. The recent rise of the nuclear family and lengthening of the average lifespan mean that decades of unfamiliar togetherness loom ahead for many couples after the husband retires.

Couples who weather the autumn of awareness sometimes discover new appreciation for each other when they have more time to spend together, no longer distracted by the children who have flown the nest and the elderly relatives who have passed away. However, the giant-garbage attitude is increasingly being expressed by Japanese women in action as well as in vocabulary. Marriages are splitting apart fastest among couples where the wife is in her forties, entering her jittery second adolescence with worries about her mate's approaching retirement. Divorces in this category have more than doubled in the past twenty years. The majority of all divorces are initiated by the spouse most accustomed to sorting and disposing of giant garbage; about three out of four divorce requests come from women.

urenokori Unsold Goods　　　　　　　　　　売れ残り

Although few Japanese choose to stay single for life, there is a large and devilishly clever arsenal of Japanese words for ridiculing people—specifically women—who remain unwed past the so-called marriageable age (*tekireiki*). The older unmarried woman is "unsold merchandise" (*urenokori*), as opposed to the brides who found themselves a "market" (*urekuchi*). She has become a "widow without going" (*ikazu goke*), a play on the popular term for marrying, "to go as a daughter-in-law" (*yome ni iku*). She is "distant from connection" (*endoi*). An almost literal equivalent of old maid is the slightly old-fashioned *rojo*. Some people tried to phrase her embarrassing situation politely in a foreign tongue by calling her "old miss" (*orudo misu*) and then, after that also began to sound insulting, "high miss" (*hai misu*). None of these words refers to bachelors, who can be described in Japanese only with a few words adopted from other languages, such as the English *bacheraa* and the Korean *chongaa*.

One anxiety shared by many women who stay single for life is the fate of their remains after death. According to Japanese funeral customs, women are laid to rest in the family grave of their husband. A woman deemed "unsold merchandise" may have trouble entering the family grave beside her parents if, for example, her older brother's wife opposes it. About 250 women, mostly those whose would-be husbands lost their lives in World War II, have solved this problem by banding together in the Women's Monument Group. They built a funeral monument near Kyoto in 1979 for the repose of their souls, and they gather there annually to honor members who died during the year.

To be called "unsold merchandise" implies that the woman waits as passively as a grocery-store tomato hoping a customer will buy it before it rots. This may have reflected reality in feudal times, but contemporary Japanese women, who have the legal right to decide if and when they marry, are evidently looking for a word that conveys a more upbeat image of single life. Women's fashion magazines have seized upon the swinging English word "singles" (*shinguruzu*) to describe both women and men. Like the English original, *shinguruzu* can apply to not only young people, but also the leftovers who never got hitched, the divorcees who left their marriages, and the bereaved left behind when their spouses die. *Shinguruzu* was the title of a Japanese comic in the mid-1980s about a family of singles: grandmother, mother, and four kids. Whenever one member's romantic involvement threatened their uniform singlehood, the rest got upset.

Japanese Word Index

139

Index

（新装版）日本語の中のおんな
Womansword

2002年6月28日　第1刷発行

著　者　キトレッジ・チェリー
発行者　野間佐和子
発行所　講談社インターナショナル株式会社
　　　　〒112-8652　東京都文京区音羽1-17-14
　　　　電話　03-3944-6493（編集部）
　　　　　　　03-3944-6492（営業部・業務部）
　　　　ホームページ　http://www.kodansha-intl.co.jp
印刷所　大日本印刷株式会社
製本所　大日本印刷株式会社

落丁本、乱丁本は、講談社インターナショナル業務部宛にお送りください。送料小社負担にてお取替えいたします。なお、この本についてのお問い合わせは、編集部宛にお願いいたします。本書の無断複写（コピー）は著作権法上での例外を除き、禁じられています。

定価はカバーに表示してあります。

© 講談社インターナショナル株式会社 1987
Printed in Japan
ISBN4-7700-2888-1